WOLFGANG ECKE

THE CASE OF
THE HIGH-RISE ROBBERY

There are over twenty intriguing cases for super sleuths to solve in this collection. Each story has a different type of crime, and a different background, and some are more tricky than others. There's a wide range of villains to pit your wits against, from an Australian widow to a chocolate thief, or a pickpocket to a door-to-door salesman. It's great fun working out which of the clues have been left deliberately and which will *really* help you nail the villain. Once you've done that, check your own conclusions with the solutions at the back of the book.

See how good you are, Super Sleuths!

WOLFGANG ECKE

THE CASE OF
THE HIGH-RISE ROBBERY

Illustrated by Rolf Rettich

Translated from the German
by Stella and Vernon Humphries

A Magnet Book

Also by Wolfgang Ecke in Magnet Books

THE MAGNET DETECTIVE BOOK 1
THE MAGNET DETECTIVE BOOK 2
THE MAGNET DETECTIVE BOOK 3
THE CASE OF THE BANK HOLD-UP

First published in Great Britain 1983
by Methuen Children's Books Ltd
Magnet paperback edition published 1984
by Methuen Children's Books Ltd
11 New Fetter Lane, London EC4P 4EE
Originally published in Germany by
Otto Maier Verlag Ravensburg
in volumes entitled:
Das Schloss der roten Affen, Der Mann in Schwarz, Das Gesicht an der Scheibe, Solo für Melodica, Das Haus der 99 Geister, Schach bei Vollmund and *Der unsichtbare Zeuge*

Printed in Great Britain
by Cox & Wyman Ltd, Reading

ISBN 0 416 47190 0

Contents

*	easy
**	quite difficult
***	difficult

I · The high-rise robbery

Tom Lipman replaced the receiver. He plumped down in the worn leather armchair beside his bed and started thinking.

One thing was clear. He couldn't do a job like that without help. He needed a partner.

He thought of all the crooks he knew, the big-time boys and the petty thieves. But the more he thought, the harder it became to make up his mind. It was far from easy to find the right accomplice. Certain risks would have to be taken which could not be ignored.

He was on the point of giving up the whole idea when a name suddenly occurred to him: Sam Lugg, always known by his nickname Smoky Sam because he was never seen without a pipe in his mouth.

Five minutes later, Lipman was at the wheel of his ramshackle old Ford, driving towards Singlewood, where Lugg lived in a wooden house near some allotments. As well as gardening, Lugg had another hobby, as it were: he was a burglar.

Sam Lugg was sitting outside his house, deep in thought chewing the stem of his curved pipe, when Lipman pulled up. Rumour had it that he never took his pipe out of his mouth, not even when he went to bed.

'Hallo Tommy,' he greeted Lipman, the pipe firmly between his teeth.

'Hallo Sam!'

Lipman sat down near Sam and went straight to the point. 'Are you still up to it, Sam?'

'Of course!'

'I've three thousand to hand out.'

'Difficult?'

'Not so much difficult as awkward.'

Smoky Sam's face fell. He disliked anything that wasn't easy. His empty pipe bobbed up and down between his lips as he took another one from his pocket and set about filling it with slow, deliberate movements. 'Come on, Tommy. Out with it! What's the game?'

And Tom Lipman told him. 'You know Omeda House in Victoria Street? I thought you would. There's an art dealer on the top floor – pictures and statues, that kind of thing. It's called Gallery Lacoste. Ever heard of it?'

Lugg shook his head. 'Not my line.'

Lipman continued: 'They sell paintings, fancy china, that sort of stuff. My client wants us to steal a set of pictures for him. There are seven that go together.'

'Are they big?' asked Lugg dubiously.

'No, quite small, about thirty centimetres square. No weight, not really.'

'What's the security system?'

'There are two doors fitted with burglar alarms connected straight to the police station. But we wouldn't use the doors. We'd go in through a window.'

Smoky Sam shook his head. 'I thought you said it's on the top floor.'

'Right. The eleventh to be precise.'

'Phew! What the devil. . . .'

'We'd get in from the roof. Let down a rope ladder and open a window.'

Lugg shook his head, mulling it over. 'Eleventh floor!' he muttered.

'Roof . . . rope ladder . . . I'm a burglar, not a circus performer! When's it supposed to take place?'

'Saturday night!' Lipman was getting impatient. 'Well? Can I count on you? Or shall I find someone else?'

Again Lugg's pipe swayed slowly up and down. 'Oh well, I can't afford to pass up three grand. I'll do it.'

'Done! Pick me up at my house just before midnight.'

It was first thing on Sunday morning, twenty past midnight to be exact, when Lipman and Lugg reached Omeda House in Victoria Street.

For an expert like Sam, sixty seconds was enough to pick the lock of the door at the back of the building. Although no one lived there except an old caretaker in the basement, the intruders decided it was safer not to use the lift. There were two hundred and forty-two steps to climb before they reached the iron door leading to the roof space. Lugg managed to force this lock in record time; in fact, he needed only eighteen seconds.

At 00.49 they stepped out onto the flat roof of the tall block. Sam had butterflies in his stomach as he saw the small moving lights of passing cars fifty metres below.

Lipman secured the rope ladder to a chimney stack and gave Lugg the signal to go first.

Pipe in mouth and lying on his stomach, Smoky Sam worked his way little by little over the edge of the roof until his feet found the top rung of the rope ladder. His face was pouring with sweat, he was so nervous. Two minutes later he found himself level with one of the large windows of Gallery Lacoste. At exactly 1 am, all was ready. By cutting a hole in the glass, he was able to reach the window handle and open the casement inwards.

Smoky Sam was working his way over the window-sill into the gallery when Tom Lipman began the three-metre descent to join him.

Five past one.

Lipman and Lugg stood among glass cases, table displays of works of art, statues and walls covered with paintings. Lipman shone his torch all around until the beam rested on a large oil painting entitled *The Glutton*. Beneath it were hung a set of seven much smaller pictures, the ones they were being paid to steal.

'There they are, Sam,' whispered Lipman.

They worked in silence and by two o'clock the pair of scoundrels, Lipman and Lugg, had left Omeda House, reversing the route they had used to enter it.

* * *

Monday, 9 am.

Brian Lacoste was, as usual, the first to arrive at the art gallery. And, as usual, he went straight to his office to put down his briefcase and to change the calendar. And to switch off the burglar alarm.

Next, he walked across to the showroom. But the moment he opened the door he stopped dead. Seven lighter patches on the wall beneath the picture of the glutton indicated an unmistakable fact. And the broken window took his breath away, although for only a moment.

Luckily, Brian Lacoste was not only an expert on works of art, he also knew correct police procedure. So he locked the showroom door and made straight for the telephone.

'I haven't been inside the room,' he assured the policemen who arrived within ten minutes. He unlocked the door for them.

It was getting on for one o'clock that afternoon when Lugg was arrested. Lipman was picked up about two hours later.

Lipman and Lugg had only their own carelessness to blame for the fact that the police found them so quickly. They themselves were kind enough to provide the one clue needed.

What was this clue? The illustration will tell you.

2 · The castle of the red gorillas

Some of the leading citizens of the French town of St Lermain used to meet every Friday evening at the Black Rose Hotel for a drink and a chat. They did so as usual on 12 May last year, a date none of those present was likely to forget in a hurry.

Around the table on that memorable night were Gustave Lerron, the chemist; Michel Jonas, the mayor; the chief constable, Victor Collet; the owner of the supermarket, Robert Roche; and an insurance agent, Marc Loire. The headmaster of the boys' school, Charles Lupont, joined them later.

They had been talking quietly for about half an hour when Lerron, the chemist, tapped his glass for silence. 'Gentlemen! If no one has any objection, I'd like to suggest a way of making our weekly gatherings more interesting.' His lively eyes darted all around, eager to see what the others had to say.

Robert Roche was the first to reply. 'I must say I don't find these meetings of ours too dull, Gustave. But if you've had a brainwave, let's hear it. Tell us what it is, and as good democrats we'll vote on it.'

There was general laughter and everyone seemed

to agree with Roche.

Lerron cleared his throat. 'I've been thinking that it might be amusing if, week by week, we took turns to tell a story,' he began. 'Anything would do, something that had happened to the speaker, say, or an incident told him by someone else. What do you all think?'

'Hm,' grunted Collet, the chief constable.

'I've no objection . . .' mumbled the mayor.

Marc Loire, however, a man with plenty to say for himself, grinned slyly.

'You know what's behind all this, don't you?' he chuckled. 'Gustave's heard some tale or other which he's dying to tell us about. It's only to justify himself that he wants us all to follow suit.' He raised his glass and took a sip. 'If you want my opinion, I'd say Charles should begin. After all, as a schoolmaster he's paid to tell the children fairy tales.'

The mayor however sided with Lerron. 'I see no reason why Gustave shouldn't kick off. I'm all for it.'

'So am I,' said Robert Roche.

Collet too nodded enthusiastically.

Gustave Lerron clapped his hands together, pleased at the outcome. 'You're outvoted, Marc,' he declared with a broad smile. 'And as you're always telling us how brave and enterprising you are, I'm going to tell you a tale that will make even your hair stand on end.'

Loire bristled. 'You do exaggerate sometimes, Gustave,' he said with an impatient wave of his hand. 'But in one sense you're quite right. I simply don't know what fear means. If you ask me, only stupid people are ever afraid.'

Such a chorus of protests greeted these words that for a few moments no one could hear himself speak.

In the end it was Charles Lupont, the headmaster, who voiced the general opinion. 'My dear Marc, fearlessness isn't always a sign of strength. Indeed, I'd go further. I believe there are times when every sensible person knows what it is to be afraid.'

Marc was highly offended. 'In other words, Charles, you consider me a fool, do you?'

'I'm sure he meant nothing of the sort, Marc,' said the mayor, trying to keep the peace. 'You mustn't take Charles so literally. But no more arguing now. Let's hear this spine-chiller of Gustave's instead. Do begin.'

'Hear, hear!' said the others, and the chemist needed no more persuasion.

'You might call my story: Alone with seven red gorillas,' he began.

'You call that a title?' objected Collet incredulously.

'What's wrong with it?' retorted Lerron. 'One title's as good as another.'

'I disagree with you, Victor,' interrupted Roche. 'I'd call it a very striking title.'

The chemist thumped his fist on the table so hard that the glasses tinkled. 'Am I to get on with it, or would you rather fight over the title?'

'We're all ears,' the mayor assured Lerron, a twinkle in his eye. He rearranged himself in his chair and adopted the pose of an eager listener as if he were acting a part on the stage.

The others too turned to Lerron expectantly, curious to hear what he had to say.

'A traveller from one of the big drug firms visits my shop regularly, and this adventure befell him the other day on the way from Paris to Orléans. His name is André Passou.

'He was driving along in his car when without any warning both his rear tyres burst. It was only six kilometres to the next village, but he was carrying such a large quantity of medical supplies that he couldn't leave the car unattended. All he could do was to sit there and wait for someone to pass that way.

'But everything seemed bewitched. The road was utterly deserted: not a car, not a cyclist, not even a pedestrian could be seen. Passou was almost in despair. At long last – and it was well after nightfall by now – an old woman appeared on the scene. She listened to André's tale of woe in stony silence, but in the end she promised she'd go and get help sent to the stranded traveller.

'Again Passou was alone, and time seemed to drag endlessly. Suddenly he jumped. From the distance he heard the unmistakable *clip clop* of horses' hoofs. And he was right. A waggon drawn by two horses came into view, driven by a man dressed all in black. The man explained that no one locally could fix the tyres before the following morning, so he invited Passou to go with him to Castle Loupou, where he could spend the night.

'Although André had never heard of the place, he didn't hesitate. He and the waggoner transferred his belongings from the car to the cart and only fifteen minutes later they passed through the castle gate. It closed behind them with a resounding clang.

'André could make out nothing of the castle except its outline. But soon they were indoors, and the man in black led him along echoing corridors, through vast halls and huge rooms which had only one thing in common: they were all empty. No furniture, no pictures, no carpets, nothing. At last they came face to face with a high wide door to which the waggoner put his ear, listening intently. As he did so, a piercing shriek was heard from within.

'André Passou gasped and he felt his blood run cold. For his guide, however, the cry appeared to be a kind of signal. Without a word he thrust open the door and motioned to Passou to pass in front of him.

'Trembling, he staggered forward. He was so frightened he could feel the sweat running down his back.

'He found himself in an enormous room in which hundreds of tallow candles were burning. In the middle was a table. It was lavishly set for two people, with fine china, antique silver cutlery and rare cut-glass, to say nothing of an abundance of mouth-watering dishes. Only one thing was missing, a host or hosts. Remembering the dreadful scream he had heard, André turned to his guide to beg him to explain the mystery . . . but the man had simply vanished.

'Passou was about to dash for the door when it re-opened and a very old gentleman entered. His

hair was snowy white and he looked as if he had stepped out of an old painting. "My dear sir, please sit down and consider yourself my guest," he said, and taking André gently but firmly by the arm he led him to the table.

'Time and again, Passou tried to start a conversation, but he had no success. The only replies the old gentleman ventured were: "Do have some caviare. . . . Why not try the lobster? . . . This breast of turkey is quite delicious, I assure you. . . ."

'So passed the next half hour, during which André had ample time to regret bitterly ever having come to Castle Loupou.

'Presently the white-haired gentleman opened

another bottle of wine. It was pinkish in colour, the kind known as rosé. As good as it was, Passou thought it left a peculiar taste in his mouth. All at once his host's face seemed to crease into a mocking sneer. Passou, greatly puzzled, felt compelled to ask the man for some explanation. But try as he might he found his teeth were so tightly clenched that he couldn't even open his mouth. Some strange change was taking place in his body, his legs and arms grew as heavy as lead and the edges of the figure opposite blurred and wavered before his eyes, first slowly, then faster and faster.

'André Passou stared helplessly as, with a soft whinnying laugh, the old man opposite him rose to his feet and moved towards the door. He stood beside it and clapped his hands smartly, his fingers edging towards the light switch. Passou gazed at the door and the blood froze in his veins. Two gigantic gorillas, their shoulders hunched, were loping towards him, lurching from side to side. It wasn't this alone that terrified him so. It was the yellow gleam of their protruding teeth; and, worst of all, the fact that their shaggy fur was bright scarlet. . . .

'"Can . . . can there be . . . such animals . . . as . . . as red . . . gorillas?" he asked himself, and it cost him a huge effort to form each word in his mind.

'In a trice, both animals were stooping over him and for a few seconds he could smell their hot stinking breath. Imagine his horror when he saw the white-haired gentleman flick the switch and all around was pitch black. Passou felt himself sinking to the ground and he lost consciousness.

‘When Passou awoke he was lying on a bed, but he couldn’t make out where it stood for there was no vestige of light anywhere. It took him the best part of a minute to recall the sinister events so far. Then he cringed in terror. Something heavy had placed itself across his legs. Cautiously André raised the upper part of his body and his hand groped forward. But a moment later he plucked it back as abruptly as if he had thrust it into a naked flame. What he had felt was coarse animal fur. . . . There was no mistake possible. One of the red gorillas was keeping watch over him.

'He lay still. His senses were sharpened and he listened hard for any tell-tale sound. His ears registered a subdued whistling on his right, like a person breathing in his sleep. The same sound could be heard on the left as well. . . . Could there be other victims there besides himself?

' "Hallo!" he called softly into the darkness. "Is there anyone here?"

'No answer.

' "Hallo!" he repeated, stretching out his left hand. The heavy breathing stopped abruptly and a shrill piercing yell rang through the darkness, echoing against the walls. Something gripped André's hand and strong claws seemed to bore into the back of it. A hairy something glided across his face. The beat of his heart was almost too painful to bear.

'He jerked his hand free and, shaking all over, held his breath as if expecting the brute to attack him. Yet nothing happened. . . .

'After an hour or so, the animal lying across his legs changed its position. It slid down from the bed and André heard the dull thud as the heavy body landed on the ground and the tap of its paws against what could only be a stone floor. Its self-satisfied grunts made Passou shudder.

'It was then that his eye caught sight of a small patch of light on a wall. It must be a window, so

André knew that day was breaking. After another twenty minutes he found he could make out a few more details. But they did nothing to encourage him. His bed stood in a very large room. And around it lay seven apes, seven fully grown gorillas, all seven with identical bright scarlet fur.

'Ten minutes later still, André worked out that his room must be at ground level. He distinctly recognised the castle wall through the window, as well as the narrow iron gate through which he had come the night before. He also saw a tree trunk.

'André eyed the gorillas. They appeared to be fast asleep. Cautiously he drew up his legs. With even greater care he swung them over the edge of the bed until he could feel the floor firmly beneath his feet. Oh no! A spring creaked! Passou stopped dead. But the beasts must have been sleeping even more soundly than he had thought possible. He judged the distance from the bed to the window to be between twelve and fifteen metres. . . .

'Everything seemed to go smoothly.

'He was no more than three paces from the window when one of the scarlet apes gave a loud howl. As if at a word of command, the other six gorillas jumped up and joined in the infernal hullabaloo, which echoed round and round the room.

'Half crazed with fear, Passou bounded to the window and stretched out his hand to open it. But it had no handle and needed a special key to open it. He turned around, cornered. He was so paralysed with fear that instead of a cry for help only a strangled gurgle escaped from his throat.

'Rearing to its full height, the largest ape was

only a few metres away from him. The other six, not much slower, were now closing in on him in a half circle.... Noiseless, unhurried, step by step....

'The leader drew itself up, ready to pounce, when a brusque order rang out through the room like a whiplash. Framed in the doorway stood the waggoner who had driven André to the castle the previous evening. In a matter of seconds the room, except for André and the bed, was quite empty....

'Had it been real, or nothing but a devilish nightmare of his imagination?

'When Passou reached the drive in front of the building, he saw his own car waiting there for him. The tyres had been fixed and the man in black was placing Passou's cases beside it.

'At the same time, the white-haired gentleman appeared at the door and walked over to André.

' "My dear sir," he said, "I know you can scarcely be pleased to see me again and I'm extremely sorry for causing you such distress. At the same time I should like to thank you in the name of science for having helped us in our research into human behaviour under stress. As compensation for the high degree of fear you have suffered, allow me to offer you a fee of two thousand francs...." And he handed him an envelope.

'André Passou took the money without hesitation, and as he drove away his eyes wandered upwards to the window on the second floor behind which, only minutes before, he had been alone – at the mercy of seven scarlet gorillas....'

* * *

Gustave Lerron, the chemist, smiled cunningly. 'Yes, gentleman, that's my story. I hope it didn't bore any of you.'

For a while there was complete silence around the table. Lupont, the headmaster, was the first to speak. 'In my opinion, such experiments are extremely sinister,' he said gravely. 'But I can't for the life of me see why the gorillas in the story had to be bright red. I've never in all my born days heard of scarlet gorillas.'

'Scientists often have the weirdest ideas,' said the mayor, 'but I must say I thought it was very decent of them to compensate the man so handsomely for what he'd suffered.'

Gustave Lerron turned to Marc Loire. 'And what has our hero to say to the story? How would you have behaved?' he asked, his eyes sparkling with irony.

'Your drug salesman seems to be very timid,' replied Loire scornfully. 'I dare say he'd have been just as scared if he'd been left alone with seven sparrows.'

Lerron smiled charmingly. 'That's exactly what I'd hoped you'd say, Marc. In fact, I happened to mention you to Passou and I told him that you said you were never frightened, no matter what happened.'

Loire nodded, but a shade nervously. 'At least I'd have earned my two thousand francs without making such a song and dance about it.'

'I mentioned that to Passou as well. And he in turn got in touch at once with Professor Mendelle – he's the white-haired gentleman I told you about

– and now the professor is looking forward greatly to your active cooperation.'

The deathly hush around the table lasted for several moments.

'What do you mean by my active cooperation?' enquired Marc Loire huskily.

'Simply this: Professor Mendelle is coming here to St Lermain tomorrow morning to take you back to Castle Loupou with him. . . . And the day after tomorrow you'll be two thousand francs the richer. . . .'

The colour drained from Marc's face and he threw up his hands helplessly. 'I . . . I . . . I'm so . . . so sorry,' he stammered. 'I've only just remembered . . . I have to . . . to l . . . l . . . leave town in a hurry. In fact, I must be off right away. I qu . . . quite forgot I have to pack. I must go immediately!'

Loire scurried off in such haste that he not only forgot to pay for his drinks but he also left his hat behind.

Gustave Lerron took a deep breath. 'At last!' he sighed, smiling to himself. 'I've finally taken him down a peg and shown the braggart what fear is. And I don't mind telling you, it's a very satisfactory feeling.'

Lupont leaned forward, his eyes wide with surprise. 'Do you mean to say it wasn't true, Gustave? That the whole thing was pure invention?' he asked incredulously.

'Of course it was,' nodded the unrepentant Lerron. 'As you said yourself only a moment ago, who's ever heard of scarlet gorillas?'

'A jolly good yarn,' said Collet, the chief constable, who had spoken little so far, 'and you told it splendidly, Gustave. I've only one comment to make and it comes from someone whose job it is to listen attentively to what is actually said. Next time, you must be more careful. If Marc had paid more heed, he couldn't have helped noticing that you made two important mistakes.'

'Did I?' Lerron was genuinely astonished.

'Yes, there were two of them, although they didn't have anything to do with the gorillas as such, nor with the car breakdown. Think it over. . . .'

Lerron took his words to heart. 'So I will. And in future I'll make sure there are no police officers present when I have a story to tell!'

Which were the two mistakes spotted by the chief constable?

3 · Happy Easter!

The people of Oslo were most surprised to see snow again on Easter Sunday. For weeks spring had been in the air. The city's streets and squares had been free of ice and slush, the crocuses in the parks were in full flower. And then this!

The snow started falling about mid-morning and it didn't stop for the rest of the day. By the time Easter Monday dawned, the Norwegian capital lay under a blanket of snow which was growing thicker by the hour.

Detective Inspector Laurenz from the Oslo Crime Squad was far from pleased when he was told that there was a Mr Arne Nilsson to see him. The time was 10.30 a.m. 'Why couldn't he have come in an hour and a half?' grumbled Sven Laurenz to himself. He had been on duty since the early hours and at twelve noon his colleague, Matt Osgard, would have arrived to take over from him.

And so Arne Nilsson found a not very friendly reception at police headquarters. He was too excited to notice it, though. 'I've been burgled!' he declared.

Sven Laurenz pointed to a chair. 'Please sit

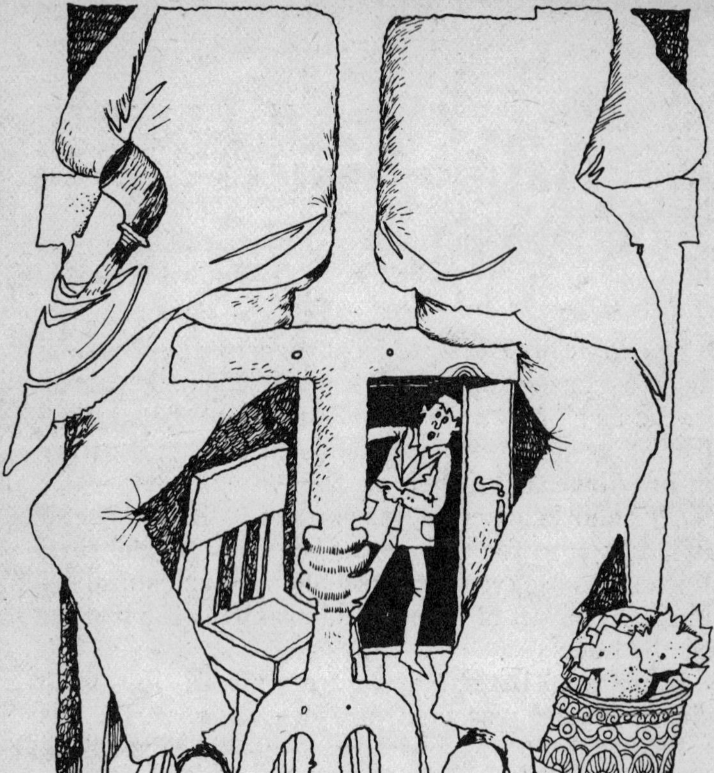

down,' he said. 'First let me have your name and your occupation and then tell me what's been stolen.'

'My name is Arne Nilsson and I'm a partner in the antique shop, Bjorn and Nilsson,' he snorted angrily. 'When I arrived at our business premises this morning....'

'But it's Easter Monday,' Laurenz interrupted him. 'Do you always go to your shop on public holidays?'

'Yes, and on Sundays too. I'm a busy man. As I was saying, I went to the shop as usual, and when I arrived I nearly had a heart attack....' For a moment he looked as if he might very well collapse, but he quickly recoverd. 'Three valuable pieces of sculpture are missing, as well as a unique diamond-studded snuffbox and a canteen of solid gold cutlery with place settings for twenty-four people. They've all vanished.'

'And how did the thieves get in?' asked Laurenz, making a few notes.

'That's the whole point, Inspector,' replied Mr Nilsson, eyeing the ceiling with a strange look on his face. 'No lock was forced, no window was broken.'

'I see from your expression that there's someone you suspect.'

'Yes,' hissed the antique dealer, his eyes sparkling. 'I suspect my partner, Knut Bjorn. He's a frivolous playboy who never has a penny to call his own. And do you know why?'

Laurenz shook his head.

'Because he gambles. Yes, Inspector, he gambles,

and I for one never trust a gambler.'

It was plain that Nilsson didn't think much of his partner. But was it only on account of the man's gambling?

'What has he said about the burglary?' asked the inspector.

'Nothing, and for one very good reason. I've not been able to ask him. I've tried to phone him at least twenty times, but there's no reply from his house.'

Laurenz looked at his watch. Just his luck! He'd have to investigate this case after all. The devil alone knew when he'd get home. . . . 'I'll get one of my men to take a statement from you,' he said flatly. 'Then I'll call and see your partner before I go to the shop. What's his address?'

It was precisely 11.45 am when Detective Inspector Laurenz reached Mr Knut Bjorn's house in a smart suburb of Oslo. He rang the bell and Bjorn himself answered the door. Bjorn was in pyjamas. He seemed genuinely shocked to hear the news.

He told the inspector that he had been fast asleep until the ring at the doorbell woke him up. And he also stated that he hadn't so much as left the house since Saturday night. 'I'd better get dressed and go to the shop with you,' he said. 'Can you give me a lift?'

Laurenz nodded. 'Certainly.'

'I've a car, of course,' Knut continued, 'but I've no car keys at the moment. I'll have to wait for the thaw before I can get them back.'

'Why is that?'

'I was careless enough to drop them in the snow somewhere between the garage and the front door, and so far I haven't been able to find them. My wife has a second set, but she's out of town and won't be back until next week.'

At the front door Knut turned around to address the police officer. 'I shouldn't be surprised if Nilsson hasn't "fixed" this burglary so as to put the blame on me,' he said softly. 'He can't understand why a fellow likes a little flutter now and again. He's convinced that one of these days I'll gamble away the entire business. He doesn't trust me an inch.'

It was getting on for 1 pm when the three men met in the antique shop, Arne Nilsson, Knut Bjorn and Detective Inspector Laurenz. So far, Laurenz hadn't been able to establish whether or not the theft had actually taken place. But one thing he knew for certain. One of the two partners had told him a lie.

The question is: Who was the liar, Nilsson or Bjorn?

4 · Dinner at the Zanzibar

With a sigh, the private detective Olaf Kellborn eased himself out of his armchair, gave the television screen one last look and went to answer the door. 'Yes? What can I do for you?' he asked the man there, who was fidgeting nervously with his hat.

'My name is Paul Oxter. I'd like a word with Mr Kellborn.'

The detective motioned to him to come inside. 'It's always a pleasure to have visitors after ten o'clock at night,' he said a trifle sarcastically.

The caller seemed most apologetic. 'I know it's late, but you're the only person who can help me.'

'I doubt that,' said Kellborn drily. 'There are dozens of private eyes here in Stockholm who'd be happy to chase even green and yellow ants for you if you offer them enough money. But step inside, have a glass of Scotch, and tell me what's worrying you, Mr Oxter.'

It was almost two minutes before Mr Oxter could collect himself and start telling his story. But he had a good listener in Stockholm's finest private detective. 'I ought to tell you first that I'm the

catering manager at the Millberg works half a kilometre down the road from here. We employ more than four thousand people on this site, and I'm also responsible for restaurants at another two of our factories. Every Friday evening, between six and seven, the managers of these restaurants bring me the week's takings. They did so as usual yesterday – it was Friday, you remember – and I locked up the money in the safe exactly as I always do.'

Kellborn interrupted his visitor. 'Do you live on the premises?'

'Yes and no. That is, I have a company flat within the works area, but there's a private entrance to it from Kolborg Street. My wife happens to be away just now – she's staying with her sister in Goteborg. This means that I normally eat out in the evening. So I left my flat at eight o'clock last night and I went into town for dinner at the Zanzibar Hotel.'

'Phew! You certainly do yourself proud!' whistled Kellborn. 'The food's fantastic. I go there myself now and then when I can afford it. But with their prices that's not very often.' He paused a moment and then continued: 'But isn't the Zanzibar rather out of your way? I'd have thought it was an awkward journey for you.'

'It's not too bad,' replied Paul, 'it takes me half an hour by car. After all, if you want a decent meal you make the effort.'

'True enough,' nodded Kellborn. 'But I didn't mean to interrupt you. Please go on.'

Again Oxter found difficulty in speaking, but after a while he pulled himself together and went on with his tale. 'It's part of my routine to walk right through the works every night to make sure it's all in order. When I got back from the Zanzibar last night I did exactly that. Everything seemed all right until I reached my office, and there I was absolutely stunned. Someone had broken into the safe.'

Kellborn pushed the bottle of whisky towards his client. 'Have another! You need it. Do you remember what time it was when you found the safe rifled?'

'Yes,' replied Oxter immediately. 'It was exactly 9.15. I remember looking at the clock, because I was about to call the police. . . .'

The detective sat up abruptly. 'Well? Why didn't you?'

Paul Oxter swallowed hard. He seemed very upset. 'Because ... because ... it would all have come out into the open. You see, I'd forgotten to lock the office door! Yes, Mr Kellborn, I'd simply forgotten to lock up, confound it. It's never happened before. . . .' At this point Oxter paused and took a folded sheet of paper from his pocket. 'I've drawn up a list of possible suspects, people who know the layout and who would also have known there were almost forty thousand krone in the safe.'

Olaf Kellborn cast his eye down the list of names. 'Are you absolutely certain that the circumstances are exactly as you've described them, Mr Oxter?' he asked searchingly.

The catering manager placed his hand on his heart. 'Yes, yes, I'm quite certain,' he replied excitedly. 'The times, the names written here are all correct. . . . But ... but ... who are you telephoning?'

'Inspector Orldag at police headquarters,' answered Kellborn with a smile. 'He'll call me all kinds of names, but late as it is he'll come out here all the same. And he'll tear your make-believe alibi to shreds, Mr Oxter. I've a feeling that somehow or other the missing forty thousand krone have found their way into your pocket.... Take it easy now, Mr Oxter. Have another nip of Scotch. The inspector won't be long....'

What made the detective realise that the catering manager had told him a pack of lies?

5 · A red-hot tip

Eddie Smedley – nicknamed Sandy, no one knew why – sat at the bar in his favourite pub, The Blue Parrot, staring gloomily into his half empty glass of beer. He cheered up in a twinkling when an old friend of his came into the pub and sat down beside him.

'Man alive!' exclaimed Sandy. 'I never expected to see you so soon, Ollie. I thought you'd got two years!'

Oliver Hall nodded. 'That's right, two years it was. But they knocked off a few months for good conduct. You know how it is. You pipe down, say "Yes sir" and "Please sir" to the screws, and then they let you out early for being a good boy.'

The barman put a pint of beer in front of him. Ollie put it to his lips and he didn't set it down again until he could see the bottom of the glass.

'What are you doing now?' asked Sandy.

Ollie lowered his voice. 'I've a red-hot tip, Sandy. Bank notes and easy stuff to unload. Feel like having a go?'

Sandy was too suspicious to hide his doubts. 'Why don't you do the job yourself?'

'Can't. The fuzz are keeping an eye on me.'

Sandy weighed it up. 'What's it worth?'

'All in all, ten thousand, I'd say. Six for you and four for me.'

Sandy shook his head. 'Seven for me, three for you.'

Ollie Hall signalled to the barman. 'Forget it, Sandy,' he whispered. 'I'll soon find someone who'll do it for six. I've too much at stake as it is to let it go for less.'

Sandy made up his mind. 'Okay, Ollie. Seeing as it's you, and you're just out of the nick. How, when and where?'

Hall shifted his chair closer to Sandy's. 'Tonight. Take the bus as far as Simbrook, to the new estate they're building in King Henry Avenue. They're still making up the road and there's no street lighting yet. Most of the houses aren't quite finished, but one row of four is already occupied. Number twenty-four belongs to a chap named Mellor. He's away on holiday and he won't be back till tomorrow. You can't force the front door – there's a special security lock fitted – but if you stand on a few bricks you can easily cut a hole in the kitchen window. Mellor keeps his cash and other valuables in an old carved chest in the dining-room.'

'In the dining-room?' echoed Sandy. 'You must be joking.'

'No I'm not. This Mellor fancies himself as a clever dick and I've heard him myself telling everyone within earshot that no burglar would ever look for cash there. He's too clever by half, if you ask me. What do you think?'

Sandy nodded. He agreed with Ollie, but he still wanted to be sure that there were no snags. 'And it's really foolproof, is it?' he persisted.

Ollie sounded quite offended. 'I wouldn't pull your leg, Sandy, not with four thou. at stake. Here, pal, you've an hour to spare. Time for another one. Cheers!'

In fact, they found time for another three pints. And between The Blue Parrot and the bus stop Sandy managed to pass four more pubs and have a drink at each of them. Now he was in the right mood.

He took the bus to Simbrook, got out at the correct stop, and with light springy steps he made his way to nearby King Henry Avenue. The new estate was still under construction, exactly as Ollie had said, and he had no trouble in discovering the row of four completed houses.

As he approached his goal he started humming softly. By placing three breeze blocks one on top of the other he found he was at exactly the right height to cut a neat circle in the kitchen window, using the glass cutter he always carried with him. He pushed in the large disc without bothering to be quiet. Still humming merrily, he reached through the hole and opened the window from the inside. He was still humming as he climbed into the kitchen.

A few moments later he was feeling his way along the hall and groping for the light switch. Suddenly the whole place was lit up, as if of its own accord.

On the landing stood a man, and he was pointing a shotgun at Sandy. 'What do you think you're doing?' he shouted in a very angry voice.

23
24
25
26

Sandy stared as if he had seen a ghost. 'I ... I ... thought you were. ... You weren't coming home till. ...' Muttering to himself, Sandy backed into the kitchen as the man advanced on him down the stairs.

'You can tell that to the police when they arrive,' barked the man with the gun. 'Sit down over there.' He pushed a kitchen stool towards the puzzled Sandy. 'The sergeant said he'd be here immediately.'

Sandy collapsed on the stool, crestfallen. 'Where did I go wrong?' he mumbled over and over again. 'That's what I'd like to know. ...'

Where had *Sandy gone wrong? What was his mistake? To find out, examine the illustration carefully.*

6 · A road accident

It was 27 April 1978.

The clock from the church tower was striking ten when the accident happened in Byron Street. Two metres from a zebra crossing, an elderly lady was hit by a car and thrown to the ground. As usual on such occasions, the statements of the shocked eye-witnesses were wildly exaggerated and one contradicted the other. Some spoke of the reckless driving of the man at the wheel, while others declared that the victim had shown complete disregard for her own safety.

An ambulance took the injured woman to the nearest hospital, and the car driver had to go with the policeman who had been summoned to the scene. He did so under protest, maintaining he was innocent. When they reached the nearby police station, the unfortunate man was taken to the duty room.

'Please sit down and show me your driving licence,' said Sergeant Kelly, pushing a chair towards the pale and trembling figure.

The man sat down heavily and mopped his forehead with his handkerchief. 'It really wasn't

my fault,' he insisted. 'The woman stepped straight into the road without looking left or right. . . .'

The police sergeant nodded and opened the man's driving licence. 'We'll make a note of all you say,' he promised. 'You're Mr Hulbert, I see.'

'Yes . . .'

'Your full name, please.'

'Peter Frederick Hulbert. I've been a travelling salesman for Greene's, the knitwear firm, for the last seventeen years and I've never had an accident in all that time.'

Kelly nodded. 'And the date of birth here, 19 March 1950, is correct?'

'Yes, that's right.'

'What about the address, 18 Kennedy Close? You're still there, I take it?'

'Yes, I haven't moved. . . . But I sounded my horn, Officer. I don't like doing that . . . it often frightens people, don't you think . . .? But there must be witnesses who heard me hoot. . . .'

Large beads of sweat kept forming on Hulbert's forehead so that he was constantly dabbing them away. He seemed to be exceptionally upset. His eyes looked feverish and his voice was hoarse as he assured Sergeant Kelly: 'This is the first time in my life that I've had anything to do with the police. I hope you've taken the addresses of the passers-by. . . .'

The sergeant waved his notebook. 'It's all down here,' he answered. 'Names, addresses and statements.'

'Surely they all said I'm completely innocent. . . . It isn't always the driver's fault. There are careless pedestrians too.'

'There are indeed,' agreed the policeman. 'And if they break the law they can be punished as well, don't you worry.'

Hulbert shrugged his shoulders helplessly.

The officer pointed to the door. 'Will you kindly wait outside for a few minutes? I want to telephone the hospital.'

'Yes, yes, of course. Do ask how the poor woman is. I'm very sorry, although it was no fault of mine. Perhaps she can be asked to confirm my innocence . . . if she's well enough to talk. . . .'

Hulbert tottered from the duty room, his knees trembling. The sergeant's glance that followed the agitated salesman was particularly thoughtful. As soon as the door was closed, Kelly picked up the phone. 'Kelly here,' he said to the receptionist. 'Get me Greene Brothers, knitwear manufacturers. . . . No, I haven't their number, but it'll be in the book.'

In less than two minutes he was through to the company's personnel officer. Kelly's approach was calm and matter-of-fact. 'It's nothing serious, Mr Shotter. A salesman of yours, a Mr Hulbert, has been involved in an accident. I only want to ask you how long he's been with your firm.'

'One moment while I look up his file, please.'

Papers rustled at the other end of the line. Then Mr Shotter's voice could be heard again. 'He's been on our payroll for seventeen years.'

'And may I ask if you're satisfied with his work?'

'What an odd question! It's hardly likely we'd have kept him on for seventeen years if we weren't satisfied. In fact, Mr Hulbert is our best and most hard-working salesman, and we'd be sorry if he left.'

'Thank you, sir. That's all I want to know.'

Kelly's next call was to the hospital. 'Put me through to casualty, please.'

This second conversation lasted four minutes. Peter Hulbert was summoned back to the duty room.

'How is the lady, Officer?'

'There's no cause for alarm, Mr Hulbert. It's a compound fracture, but the doctor thinks she'll be on her feet again in about six weeks.'

'Thank goodness for that!' said Mr Hulbert, again wiping his brow.

'And now we come to the second point,' the sergeant continued.

Hulbert was completely taken aback. 'The second point? What else can there be? Is there some new evidence against me?'

Sergeant Kelly shook his head. 'Not on the reckless driving charge, if that's what you mean.'

Peter Hulbert stared. The colour had drained from his face. 'But . . . but . . . what else can it possibly be?' He could barely speak.

'We'll have to go to another part of the building, I'm afraid. You'll soon find out what's wrong.'

'But where? I don't understand a word you're saying, Officer.'

Kelly paused before answering. 'We're going to the CID, Mr Hulbert.'

Hulbert's face turned grey. His arms drooped helplessly. 'The CID?' he whispered, scarcely audible.

'Yes. I regret to say that there's something very fishy about the driving licence in your possession. Unless I'm very much mistaken, it looks as if it's been falsified. . . .'

Why did Sergeant Kelly suspect that Hulbert's driving licence had been tampered with? What was wrong with it?

7 · Chicken and mushroom pie

Graham Oswald shot up in bed, only half awake. The telephone again! He glanced at the alarm clock as he climbed out of the warm sheets. It was 4 am.

The last call had been a little after 3 am. Grim-faced, Graham stamped through the flat and seized the receiver. 'Yes?' he barked into the mouthpiece.

'Chicken and mushroom pie. Take four pieces of chicken, wash and dry them thoroughly . . .'

Graham Oswald slammed down the receiver, his cheeks red and mottled. He was absolutely livid.

Six hours later, Graham sat facing Inspector Howe. The police officer gave a brief summary of what he had just been told. 'You say that for the last three nights you've been disturbed several times by mysterious phone calls. And that whenever you answer the phone, you hear a voice reading out cookery recipes?'

'Not recipes,' Graham interrupted. 'It's only one, and it's always the same. A recipe for cooking ch . . . ch. . . .' He had to swallow hard before he could complete the sentence: 'For cooking chicken and mushroom pie.'

The inspector nodded. 'You also say that you find chicken in any form particularly distasteful?'

Graham shuddered. 'I can't stand it. The very word makes me feel sick.'

'I understand, Mr Oswald. Can you tell me who knows about this strong dislike of yours?'

'No one. Or at least, now I come to think of it, I must have mentioned it at the office. But that was years ago. . . . The whole thing baffles me. How can there be an Ansaphone at the other end of the line whenever the phone rings and when I haven't even dialled?'

'Are you sure it *is* an Ansaphone?' enquired the inspector.

'Yes, I'm certain. You know the telephone service Dial-a-Dish? Well, the day before yesterday I dialled them, and I got the same voice using identical words. The only difference was that the sound was much sharper when I dialled myself.'

'Have you had a telephone long?'

'No, it was installed only a week ago.'

'I suppose the people you work with know you're on the phone now?' suggested Howe.

Graham nodded gloomily.

'Do you think they have anything to do with it?'

'I simply can't say. The first time it happened I told them about it, but they only laughed at me.'

That afternoon, Inspector Howe questioned Graham's three office colleagues, one at a time. Here are his notes on what they said:

Hope: Yes, I know Graham had a phone installed recently. No, we're not exactly friends. His dislike of chicken? I can't remember ever having heard of it. How odd . . .! No, you wouldn't catch me getting up in the middle of the night to find a call-box in order to play a practical joke on Graham. In any case, I always sleep like a log. . . .

Benson: Ha! Ha! You can say that again, Inspector! I'm always ready for a lark! Now that you mention it, our dear friend Oswald did mention once how much he loathes chicken. . . . Yes, I'm on the phone at home. . . . Indeed I did, in the old days . . . I used to enjoy playing about with tapes, but I gave it up long ago. You grow out of that kind of thing, don't you?

Smith: No, Inspector, we aren't on the phone. . . . If you ask me straight, I have to admit that I don't much care for Graham as a person. He's so fussy about petty details. . . . You want to know what I think about those phone calls of his? To be frank, I believe he's making the whole thing up ... although now I come to think of it imagination isn't exactly his strong point.... Do you mean to say a person can actually pick up a phone and dial for a recipe? Well, I didn't know that!'

These interviews left Inspector Howe in no doubt at all that one of Graham's three colleagues was the culprit. When challenged, the man confessed immediately that he had been responsible for the night-time telephone hoax.

Which of the three was it?

8 · Dirty work at the car-park

The large public car-park outside the Town Hall had room for a hundred and eighty vehicles. It was divided into Blocks A, B, C and D, each manned by a full-time attendant. Since they shared the work equally, each of the four attendants had forty-five parking spaces to look after.

The entrances were separate from the exits. The parking fee was fixed according to the length of time the car would be parked; it was paid on the car's arrival.

It was 7.45 am precisely when a grey Metro drove into Block B. The car was the first to arrive at that Block and, indeed, the rest of the car-park was almost empty.

A man with a big bushy beard and sunglasses got out of the Metro. He wore a checked peaked cap and a light raincoat. He locked his car carefully and beckoned to the Block B attendant, Alfred Whicker.

'What's happened?' asked the customer. 'Why aren't there any cars here?'

Alfred Whicker grinned. 'In half an hour there won't be a single space left. You're lucky you could get here so early. How long will you be leaving the car for, sir?'

The Metro driver wasn't quite sure. 'I shan't be back before eleven o'clock,' he said vaguely.

So Alfred Whicker told him how much it would be for four hours' parking, the driver paid and was given an official receipt.

8.30 am.

As the attendant had predicted, the Town Hall car-park was absolutely full. To the right of the Metro was parked a dark red Mercedes sports car. Ten minutes earlier, a white Escort had pulled into the space to the left.

Not far away, a man had his eyes glued on the area concerned. He watched closely everything that was going on in the neighbourhood of the Metro. He wore a brown suede jacket and a deerstalker hat. A curved pipe was clenched firmly between his teeth. Only the most acute observer would have realised that this man in country clothes was in fact the very person who had left the grey Metro, but now wearing different outer garments.

8.40 am.

This seemed to be the moment the man in the brown jacket was waiting for. While the attendant was busy taking money at the far end of Block B, he sprang into action. Swiftly, but without drawing attention to himself, he approached the grey Metro.

Thirty seconds later the car drove off unnoticed, leaving by the usual exit.

And three minutes later still, Alfred Whicker motioned a bright yellow Volkswagen into the now empty space. It didn't worry him in the least that the Metro had left so early. After all, the driver had paid in advance for a four-hour stay.

11.10 am.

The man with the bushy beard, sunglasses and a light raincoat stormed towards Alfred Whicker. 'What's happened to my car?' he yelled.

'The Metro?' stuttered the attendant, staring at the space now taken by the yellow Volkswagen, and by this time, it so happened, flanked by another two cars of the same make.

The man in the raincoat seized Whicker by the lapels and shook him.

'I hold you responsible!' he thundered. 'There were valuable paintings in that car, as well as two sculptures which are worth thousands!'

A passing policeman hurried to the scene. 'What's going on here?' he demanded.

The bearded man released Whicker and turned to the constable. His voice was so excited that he could hardly get the words out. 'This is supposed to be a supervised car-park,' he fumed. 'If the attendants do their duty, how is it possible for a car to be stolen from here?'

The policeman couldn't think of an immediate answer.

'Listen, Officer,' continued the Metro driver, waving his hands angrily. 'I left my car here at a quarter to eight this morning. When I returned a minute ago, it had gone. Can't a man leave his car in an attended car-park for three hours or thereabouts without someone stealing it? Why do they charge us if the cars aren't safe here, that's what I

want to know. They're taking our money on false pretences!'

The man tugged at his beard while Alfred Whicker's hands grew damp with dismay. Meanwhile, the policeman tried to disperse the gathering crowd before addressing the irate driver. 'Where exactly did you leave your car, sir?'

'In the space that yellow Volkswagen's in. The cars on either side of mine were a dark red Mercedes and a white Escort. . . .'

With a glance at the ever-increasing number of inquisitive onlookers, the policeman said: 'You'd better come with me to the police station. I'll have to take statements from you both.'

Ten minutes later, at the station, the policeman set about taking down the two differing statements.

All at once, Alfred Whicker sprang to his feet, and pointing to the Metro driver he shouted furiously: 'I've got it now! The man's a liar!'

He seemed to have hit the nail right on the head, for as quick as a flash the bearded man jumped up and disappeared through the door. . . .

Alfred Whicker took a deep breath and plumped down on a chair. 'What luck that I saw through him just in time!' he said with a sigh of satisfaction. 'The mean blighter tried to be too clever, but he overplayed his hand. If he hadn't made such a crucial mistake. . . .'

What was the bearded man's mistake? We can guess that he was trying to claim his car had been stolen so he could recover the cost of the paintings and sculptures, as well as the cost of the car. But what gave the game away?

9 · Frontier incident

When did it happen? On 2 December 1981.

Where did it happen? At the customs check-point on the frontier between Austria and Germany.

There was hardly any traffic crossing from Austria into Germany on that December evening; in the last four hours, only three vehicles had gone through customs. It was very rare for things to be so slack. Not that the customs officials and frontier police were complaining. For several hours an icy wind had been blowing through the valley, with a nasty drizzle into the bargain. It was the kind of light rain that changes to sleet from time to time, too.

This peaceful spell was not destined to last long.

At 23.10 hours the phone on Sergeant Siegel's desk rang. As he listened, the information he was given was so startling that he jumped up from his chair. But before he could ask any questions the caller had rung off.

The sergeant summoned the other officers together without delay. 'I've just had an anonymous telephone call,' he explained. 'I was told that a car will be here quite soon, a Fiat with French number-plates, and that hidden inside it are supposed to be containers with ten kilogrammes of drugs. We've work to do, lads!'

The red alert was given. The frontier barrier was closed and every man on duty was ready and prepared.

The minutes ticked by slowly.

All eyes were fixed on the Austrian stretch of the valley. It was a winding road with a long succession of S-bends right up to the frontier post. At last, in the far distance, they made out a pair of headlights and close behind them was another pair. There was

no doubt about it. Two cars would soon reach the check-point.

Every now and then they would both disappear from sight, only to re-emerge.

Finally, the first car arrived and drew up in front of the customs barrier. Sergeant Siegel gave a cry . . . it was a black Fiat! And it had French number-plates.

The Fiat was beckoned into a side bay just as the second car halted. This was a dark green Opel with a German number-plate. The initial letter was M, which meant that it was registered in Munich. The driver was asked the usual: Anything to declare? And when he answered No, he and his passenger were allowed through into Germany. The officials were interested only in the Fiat.

Meanwhile, this French-registered car had been taken to the garage, where two specialists immediately went to work to check it thoroughly. The French couple who owned the car protested loud and long, but to no avail. Half an hour passed, but nothing was found.

Towards half-past midnight, two further cars pulled up, again heading for Germany. The first one was Dutch, a DAF, registered in Amsterdam. The other was a Triumph sports car, a brown one, and it carried Austrian number-plates. After they'd answered routine questions, both drivers were allowed to proceed.

It was getting on for 3 am before the disappointed customs officers, swearing under their breath, began putting the Fiat to rights again. They had found nothing whatever.

They knew now that someone had played a hoax on them.

But was that the end of the story? No!

In the early hours of that morning a car skidded off the road into a tree about twelve kilometres into Germany. The occupants were taken to hospital. While the vehicle was being recovered, several kilogrammes of hashish were found, hidden in some canisters.

An on-the-spot investigation showed that the car had crossed into Germany from Austria. And it was also confirmed that it had passed through customs after the Fiat had been stopped.

The anonymous accusation against the French-registered car turned out to be a false one. It had clearly been intended to throw the customs men off the real scent, and to keep them extremely busy at a crucial moment.

In which car were the dope smugglers: the DAF, the Opel or the Triumph?

10 · A dangerous game

Alma Honeysuckle, short, stout, and fifty-three years of age, sat sobbing on the couch in her living-room. It was in a terrible state, and she had no need to spell things out to Sergeant Popper who had been summoned to the scene. The place had been ransacked. Drawers had been emptied on to the floor, pictures torn from the walls, plants tipped out on the carpet. Old letters, books and the contents of a sewing-box were scattered everywhere.

The same chaos could be seen in the other three rooms. It looked as if a hurricane had raced through the small terraced house.

Sergeant Popper patted Mrs Honeysuckle's arm soothingly. 'There now, madam, try and calm yourself. We need a clear description of the intruders. The sooner we circulate it, the better chance our men will have of catching the villains. Please tell me what they looked like.'

With a great effort, Mrs Honeysuckle pulled herself together. 'They were between twenty and twenty-five, I'd say,' she began, dabbing the tears from her face. 'One wore a faded denim jacket and blue jeans. The other had dark trousers, a bright

yellow shirt and a corduroy jacket. Oh yes, and he wore glasses too. . . .'

'Did they speak with any particular accent?'

'I really couldn't say. I expect I was too scared to take it in if they did. But one thing I'm sure about. When they'd finished, they drove off in a battered old Mini, a light blue one.'

'That's most helpful, Mrs Honeysuckle.' Sergeant Popper seemed very pleased with the information. His colleague, who had been taking notes throughout, dashed off in a great hurry to circulate the *Wanted* notice.

Popper meanwhile tried to establish more details. 'You said you'd been to the bank to draw out £500 and that you'd come straight home afterwards. . . .'

Mrs Honeysuckle nodded. 'I only called in at the baker's on the way. You know how things are. . . . With all that cash in my handbag I didn't want to be out too long, not with all the muggings you hear about.'

'And you didn't notice the two men in the street?'

'No, not till they burst into the house. It was exactly twelve o'clock when I came in. The clock was striking as I took off my coat and put the money away in the green vase standing on the bookcase. I've hidden money in that vase for the last twenty-five years and it's always been all right till now. . . . Then I went into the kitchen to make myself some tea. I was about to light the gas when I heard a sound like a key dropping on to the floor. I turned round and there they were . . . coming straight for me. "Where's the money?" they shouted. Before I could scream, they stuffed a tea-towel into my mouth and tied me to a kitchen chair. Then they tied the chair to a pipe. . . .'

Alma Honeysuckle began sobbing again. 'I . . . I . . . I could hear them in the living-room. They were throwing everything about. I was praying hard that they wouldn't look in the vase. How could I tell my husband that the £500 had gone?

'But they found the money in the end. . . . It was two hours before I could free myself and phone you.'

Sergeant Popper didn't interrupt. He inspected the ransacked rooms once more, a knowing smile on his lips.

Half an hour later, the second police officer returned. 'Bill and Henry have combed the neighbourhood,' he said, shaking his head, 'but no one has seen either of the two men or a battered light blue Mini.'

'I'm not surprised,' said Sergeant Popper, getting to his feet. 'Mrs Honeysuckle is a charming lady, but she's also a very good story-teller and a most convincing actress.'

The woman in question stared. 'What . . . wh . . . what are you s . . . saying?' she stammered, turning as white as a ghost.

'What I'm saying is that you've made it all up. You tried to throw dust in our eyes, but unfortunately for you you tripped yourself up.'

Alma Honeysuckle swallowed hard, but said nothing.

'I dare say it's true that you drew out the money – the bank will tell us that – but only you know why. Probably you want to buy something your husband won't approve of, and so you invented the two burglars.'

'B . . . but you can't p . . . p . . . prove it!'

The officer shook his head. 'There's no need to, Mrs Honeysuckle. You've kindly supplied the proof yourself. Telling lies isn't as easy as some people think. You've been playing a very dangerous game, though, misleading the police. . . .'

And this time, Alma Honeysuckle's tears were real enough.

This is a difficult case. To solve it we need to know what was the crucial mistake made by Mrs Honeysuckle in her statement to the police.

11 · Chocolate Charlie

Charlie Chuckles was a forger of passports and cheques. This was his line of business and the reason why he'd had more than one prison sentence in his fifty years of life. But he had also one ruling passion, and this had given him the nickname Chocolate Charlie. For he adored chocolate in any form and he could never have enough to satisfy him.

The shape, size or flavour didn't matter in the least. It could be milk chocolate, plain chocolate, coffee, orange or peppermint cream chocolate, hard centres, soft centres, fruit-and-nut or marzipan chocolate.

If he had a favourite, perhaps it was for chocolates filled with cherry brandy. But Charlie wasn't fussy. As long as it was chocolate, he would polish it off in record time and still come back for more.

In a word – or, rather, in several words – if there were chocolates to be had, Chocolate Charlie was prepared to commit any crime for them.

In fact, once a month, he used to steal enough supplies to keep him going for the next four weeks. And although the police knew of this weakness of his, they never had been able to catch him red-handed, nor had they even found a clue that would lead to his arrest.

It was 10 March.

The time had come for Charlie to re-stock with all his much-loved goodies.

Today, he decided, he would rob Chocorama, the most expensive shop of its kind, which was situated in a very exclusive New York suburb.

At twenty minutes past midnight, he got into his car.

It must have been the thought of all those mouth-watering chocolates that made him less careful than he should have been. For he failed to notice that he had been exceeding the speed limit.

It was only when a patrol car overtook him that he found himself in trouble and was fined on the spot. He nodded apologetically to show that he was sorry and, keeping his mouth tightly shut, he listened meekly to the traffic policeman's sermon about observing the law. Before he drove off, he tucked the speeding ticket into the inside band of his hat, where he had a habit of keeping important slips of paper.

At five minutes to one, he arrived at the street he wanted. It was one at right-angles to the road where Chocorama was to be found. He parked the car in the shadow of a large advertisement hoarding and took a big hold-all from the boot. The shop was only a short distance away.

By 1.10 am he had forced the two locks on the front door and was standing in the middle of the shop. A street lamp outside gave him all the light he needed. He closed his eyes for a moment, inhaling the fragrant aroma that always lingers in places where chocolates are made by hand. Then he slipped off his coat, placed his hat on a statuette and started feasting.

Charlie Chuckles ate chocolate steadily for a good half-hour. He wolfed down four outsize slabs of assorted flavours and the contents of the biggest box of liqueur chocolates he could find. Then, choosing only the finest and most expensive lines the shop had to offer, he began to fill the hold-all. This done, he thought he'd better slip a few more bars into his numerous pockets – just to be on the safe side – when he heard the wail of a police car siren.

Chocolate Charlie panicked. In a flash, he slipped on his coat, grabbed the hold-all and made his getaway by the back door, which he had wisely located on his arrival.

By 2.20 am he was safely at home, tucked up between the sheets. He could hardly have known that the police car had been on its way to a road accident, and that the break-in at Chocorama wouldn't be discovered until 8 am.

The owner of the shop rang the police as soon as he saw what had happened and before he'd even taken off his coat and beret. Two officers were on the spot by 8.20 that same morning. Then things took their inevitable course. For Charlie Chuckles, known to his friends as Chocolate Charlie, had made a serious blunder for which he had to pay the price.

He himself realised what he had done when he

saw two policemen outside his door at half-past ten. It was his own fault. He'd put the law on his tracks through sheer carelessness.

How did Chocolate Charlie give himself away? If you've read the story carefully, and also examined the illustration, you ought to be able to spot the mistake that led to his arrest.

12 · The stolen tune

James Gilbert from Washington DC was a successful stamp dealer. His hobby was the guitar and he played it very well indeed. He also wrote songs when he was in the right mood.

One September evening he was in Chicago attending a stamp exhibition. After dinner at his hotel he went for a stroll around the block.

Suddenly he stopped dead and listened hard. Over the noise of the traffic he could hear a stereo, and the tune played was strangely familiar. It sent shivers down his spine. It took him less than a minute to be a hundred per cent sure, but then he knew: the group was playing a song he had written, one that had never to his knowledge been recorded. There was no doubt about it. Someone had stolen his tune. James Gilbert did not hesitate.

He located the apartment from which the music came. Its owner was only too pleased to show him the record in question. From the sleeve he got all the details he needed about the group, the record company, the publisher and the supposed composer.

It was the composer's name that gave him a

shock. It appeared to be a certain Francis Hilton. And that happened to be the name of the manager of Gilbert's Washington stamp shop, although the man was always known as Frank.

As chance would have it, the music publishers concerned had their headquarters in Chicago. So next day, as early as he could, Gilbert called at the offices. This time, it was the company's turn to be surprised. They showed Gilbert the manuscript, written in his own hand, but signed as if it were the original work of Francis Hilton. He was shown the contract too; this also bore the same signature.

Although Gilbert was seething with rage, he kept his head. Business must come first, so he carried on with his trip, and went on from Chicago to Detroit and Boston before returning home at the end of the week.

When he was back in his Washington office, he sent for his business manager. The following conversation took place:

Gilbert: I'd no idea you were a musician, Frank.

Hilton: Pardon? I'm not a musician.

Gilbert: I'd call anyone who writes songs a musician, wouldn't you? Especially if they've been published and recorded.

Hilton: But I've never written a song in my life!

Gilbert: You never said a truer word. You only stole a song of mine and passed it off as your own work! That's known as piracy among musicians. But in your particular case, as you sold it for publication, it's stealing, Frank, just plain theft!

At this point Hilton turned deathly pale and groped for a chair.

Hilton: Only Bobby Berg could have played such a trick on me. (Berg was the firm's accountant.)

Gilbert: You're crazy! Why should Bobby do such a thing?

Hilton: He hates me. He'd stop at nothing to get me into trouble. He couldn't have guessed that you'd look up those publishers while you were in Chicago.

Gilbert: But it's your signature on the contract. I've seen it often enough to recognise it.

Hilton: He forged it.

James Gilbert paced up and down the room for a while. Then he sent Hilton away and a few minutes later he rang for the accountant, Berg.

Gilbert: Did you know I'm interested in music?

Berg: Sure. You play the guitar. Everyone knows that.

Gilbert: And what do you play?

Berg: Nothing. I'm tone deaf.

Gilbert: Is it true that you can't stand the sight of Frank?

Berg: If you want the truth, yes.

Gilbert: A song I wrote has just been published and it's been issued under Frank's name. He's suggesting that *you* did it, to get him into trouble with me.

At this point Bobby Berg also turned deathly pale and groped for a chair.

Berg: He's a liar! First of all, I've no idea where you keep the songs you write. And secondly I can't read music. I couldn't even have copied it out properly. And I wouldn't have known if it was any good in the first place.

Gilbert: And you've never been in touch with any music publishers?

Berg: Never in my life. Besides, I'd have had to forge Hilton's signature, which is a criminal offence. I'd never risk that. You could go to prison for it.

Gilbert: Okay. You may go.

James Gilbert rested his chin on his hands and thought long and hard on what he had heard. After fifteen minutes' reflection, he believed he knew which one of the two men had stolen the song he had written.

The question is this: Who was guilty of stealing James Gilbert's tune, Hilton or Berg?

13 · A message in code

The convict Hugh Wimpey, generally known as Fingers, was in a jolly and friendly mood on this particular day. He pushed the trolley of dirty laundry past Prison Warder Hubbard with such enthusiasm that you'd have thought he'd been waiting all his life for such a job. And it was this unexpected gusto that made Warder Hubbard begin to smell a rat.

Once his suspicions were aroused, he followed every movement the prisoner made out of the corner of his eye. It didn't escape his notice that as Wimpey delivered his load he brushed against the van driver not once but twice. And each time it looked as though the encounter wasn't wholly accidental.

Twenty-five minutes later, Warder Hubbard stood before the prison governor, Rupert Hunt, and handed his superior a note with an air of triumph.

'I discovered this, sir. I found it among the laundry leaving the prison in the van.'

'And who wrote it? One of our inmates, I suppose?' asked Governor Hunt, taking the note from

Hubbard's hand.

'That's right, sir. It was Fingers ... I mean to say ...' – here Hubbard corrected himself quickly when he saw the governor's disapproval – 'it was Number 192, Hugh Wimpey, in Block J. He intended to smuggle a message outside. I've already had a word on the quiet, you might say, with the

driver. And he admits that he was expected to deliver it to Wimpey's brother, who lives in Dingley.'

'Have you said anything to the prisoner?'

Hubbard shook his head and pointed to the note. 'I wanted a word with you first, sir,' he said, slightly embarrassed. 'It's written in code, as you can see. I haven't been able to crack it. Perhaps we should call in an expert.'

The governor smiled. 'We don't want to make fools of ourselves, now do we, Hubbard? Take another look at it. I think you'll be able to solve Wimpey's secret code. He's only telling his brother the time and day he'll try to escape. I'm afraid we'll have to put a spoke in his wheel.' And he handed the paper back to the warder. 'Here you are. Read it again.'

'All right. I'll have another go, if you like, sir,' mumbled the warder sourly. He'd much rather have called in an expert. But he dutifully read the words again . . . and again . . . and again.

In fact, he had to read them many times. And it was only after the seventeenth try that a smile of satisfaction lit up his face. For the last time, he examined the text:

DAY	NEXT	FREEDOM	HAVE
READY	BEFORE	TWELVE	TWO
CAR	BID	WEEK	FOUR

'I've got it!' exclaimed Hubbard, beaming. 'Yes, you're right, sir. It says everything – the exact time as well as the day. Fancy that!'

And this explains why Fingers' attempt to escape from gaol failed so sadly. He landed quite literally in Warder Hubbard's arms.

At what time and on which day did Prisoner 192 intend to escape?

14 · Super sleuth, Swedish style

Last 9 July, the Super Sleuth Club Headquarters received a letter from Falun, in Sweden. Falun is a smallish town, about two hundred kilometres north-west of Stockholm. The letter, signed Nils Dagerholm, read as follows:

I am a teacher at a village school not far from Falun. Friends of mine send me your detective stories regularly. I enjoy translating them into Swedish and giving them to my pupils to solve. They have great fun doing this. The boys and girls here are between ten and thirteen years of age.

A few weeks ago, I myself made up a story like one of yours for a rather special occasion. The children had to discover as many of my deliberate mistakes as they could. I thought you might like to see it, so here it is. Do use it, if you think it's amusing.

Kindest regards from Nils Dagerholm.

Well, we decided it was a jolly good story, so it is printed below. The only change that we made was in the title. We have called it:

SUPER SLEUTH, SWEDISH STYLE.

Here it is:

Gunnar Falk was old and so hard of hearing that without a hearing-aid he was completely deaf. All the same, he was fitter than many a man half his age. For instance, every morning except on Sundays he used to walk the five kilometres that separated his house from the nearest village and then return on foot. That meant he was clocking up a steady seventy kilometres a week in all.

Mr Falk had two passions in life. One was watching television, the other was reading and listening to detective stories. That one day he himself would be involved in a real 'whodunnit' was something he'd never have expected to happen, not even in his wildest dreams.

It was a Friday.

It had been announced that that evening, Swedish television would be showing one of the best-known thrillers from the days of silent films. So Gunnar decided that instead of his usual daily footslog into the village, he'd take the bus into town to have his hearing-aid repaired. When he got to the shop, he was terribly annoyed to discover that it would have to be sent away to the factory for repair. It wouldn't be ready for at least five days.

Well, it couldn't be helped. There was nothing for Gunnar to do except go home again without his hearing-aid.

So he was in a very bad temper when, in spite of everything, he sat down that evening in front of his television set to watch the silent film: *Murder on the Jumbo Jet*.

It was very exciting and just as a man with a lisp

was saying the words: 'I recognise you!', Gunnar's heart jumped. He distinctly heard the sound of someone trying to open his front door with a key. He leapt to his feet, tiptoed from the room and flung open the front door.

A masked man was standing there, but he was so taken aback that he offered no resistance. He allowed Gunnar to lock him in the kitchen. When the police arrived fifteen minutes later, they found the unsuccessful intruder sitting with his ear to the wall, listening spellbound to the film in the next room. The officers had their work cut out persuading him to leave the film and go with them to the waiting police car.

Well, Super Sleuths? That was the Swedish story. As Nils Dagerholm, the teacher, pointed out, it has several mistakes in it. How many of them can you find?

15 · The widow from Australia

It was 20 June 1978. That was the day when Jefferson Kirby, the chief cashier at the City Bank, Oxford, succeeded in robbing his employers of £300,000 by means of a most cunning fraud. However, clever as he was, it took only ten days for the CID's net to close in on him. He was arrested and given a heavy sentence. But the money itself was never found.

Edinburgh, 18 May 1982.

The caller eyed the beautiful, expensively furnished sitting-room into which the housemaid had shown him, with great interest. 'I'll tell madam you're here,' she said, blushing under the scrutiny of the lean young man's penetrating eyes.

Exactly five minutes later, Pamela Ferguson entered the room. She was twenty-nine years old, a pale but beautiful woman. Her sad expression was only emphasised by the cut of her elegant but plain black dress, set off by a valuable diamond brooch.

'You've come from an insurance company, I believe?'

The visitor bowed slightly. 'I'm Arthur Robbins

from the Silver Star Company in London,' he introduced himself. Even as he spoke, it crossed his mind that he had in fact spent far less time in London recently than in Oxford.

'I can't remember asking your company to send me an agent,' remarked Mrs Ferguson, her voice as charming as ever.

'I'm sorry, but there must have been some misunderstanding.' Again he gave a little bow. 'I'm not an insurance agent. I'm the company's chief detective.'

Mrs Ferguson suddenly sat bolt upright, all attention and curiosity. But not a muscle twitched in her beautiful face as she pointed to an armchair. 'Do sit down and tell me what I can do for you, Mr . . . Mr . . .' she hesitated.

'Robbins,' the detective reminded her. 'Arthur Robbins.'

He sat down, placed his fingertips together with studied care and pursed his lips. 'If I may, I'll run over the ground very briefly. You're Mrs Pamela Ferguson, you arrived in this country from Sydney, Australia, seven months ago, and you've made your home here in Edinburgh. Your husband was Paul Ferguson, a stock breeder in Parramatta, who was killed in a road accident on 26 August last year.' He looked at the lady innocently and asked: 'Have I left out anything, Mrs Ferguson?'

The woman dabbed the corner of her eye with a lace handkerchief and shook her head. Then, gazing hard at the detective, she said tearfully: 'I think you owe me an explanation, Mr Robbins.'

He agreed courteously. 'You mean that it's rather

tactless to remind a young widow of recent unhappy events when she's trying to forget them by settling somewhere completely fresh?'

She nodded. 'You've put it rather clumsily, but certainly that's how I feel.'

'I should explain, madam, that the reason for my visit comes under three headings,' he continued somewhat awkwardly. 'So far, I've dealt with one. May I tell you about the second?' Without waiting for permission, he went on: 'Almost four years ago, a certain Jefferson Kirby robbed the bank where he worked of £300,000. Although there was an army of policemen on his heels, he had the nerve to go straight to London to marry a certain Diana Balman. Just imagine, on that day of all days – first the robbery, then the wedding! A cool customer, this fellow Kirby, and a good organiser into the bargain, don't you agree? Of course he was caught, but. . . .' Robbins paused, shook his head as if baffled and, staring fixedly at the pale Pamela Ferguson, he went on with his tale. 'The case wasn't closed, however. Although Kirby was behind bars . . . sorry! I'm being tactless again. Although Kirby had been caught, the money and his young bride both vanished into thin air. Not a trace was left. Until today. . . .

'But what happens next? Ah! That's the really exciting part of the story! The organising genius Kirby got a sentence of ten years' imprisonment, but that was no use to the insurance company concerned, the Silver Star. Until, that is, my directors had a brainwave.' Here Robbins tapped his chest importantly. 'They decided to put me on the job. I was relieved of all other duties, you understand, and told to devote my time to solving the mystery.' Here he lowered his voice and his eyes flashed in triumph. 'I'm ambitious, madam. I made it my business to clear up the case. I was determined to solve the problem of the vanished fortune and the missing Mrs Kirby. Do you understand?'

There was an icy look in Pamela Ferguson's eyes. 'Why are you telling me this?' she challenged Robbins. 'Why should I allow you to ramble on with this idiotic story? Can you tell me that as well?'

'Indeed I can,' replied Robbins promptly.

'I can hardly wait!' jeered the lady coolly.

'The answer is that you are the Diana Balman whom Kirby married on 20 June 1978.'

The woman leaned forward, her lips quivering and her voice far less sweet than before. 'You must be out of your mind!' She fairly spat out the words. 'You're raving mad. I was never in Oxford in my life and I know nothing about this Mr Kirby of yours, nor of the crime he committed. You said yourself that I came from Australia only seven months ago, didn't you?'

The detective didn't deny it. 'That brings me to the third heading. It's taken me the best part of four years to track you down. My notes fill a hundred and eighty pages. . . .'

Pamela Ferguson waved his remarks aside. 'I couldn't care less!' she retorted. 'And now it's my turn to tell you something. If you don't leave this house immediately, I'll call the police.'

Robbins smiled shrewdly. 'I'm the only person investigating this case. No one else knows anything about it. For £100,000 it could remain that way.'

The widow took the receiver from the phone, then paused. 'Ask for Inspector McPherson,' grinned Robbins, trying to be helpful. 'He's the man you want.'

Pamela Ferguson did indeed ask for McPherson. Arthur Robbins had to give her credit for sheer nerve.

'Hallo? Inspector McPherson? There's a madman here . . .' she shrilled. 'He's mixing me up with someone else. I need your help!'

Robbins took the receiver from her hand. 'Okay, Jock. It's all right to come with the arrest warrant. It *is* Diana Kirby and the game's up. Yes, she gave herself away. I bet her husband will be furious when he finds out.'

The London detective was silent, listening to the reply at the other end of the line. Then he replaced the receiver.

'By the way, madam, I have more bad news for you,' he declared, and he sounded almost sincerely sorry. 'You made a very foolish mistake when you bought that passport in Sydney. Mr Ferguson's widow Pamela is an old lady of seventy-two. Not that we need that information now. . . . Come on, cheer up! We all make mistakes, you know, even the cleverest of us. McPherson will be here at any moment. . . .'

Pamela Ferguson, alias Diana Kirby, had indeed made a very serious mistake. You could say she gave herself away. What was it she said that made Arthur Robbins sure he had come to the right person?

16 · The birthday party

It was a fine evening in June. Nearly seventy guests had arrived at Michael Sylvester's house for the party. The large garden was festooned with fairy lights, and a modern string quartet played dance music on the veranda.

The party was in honour of Michael's only daughter Gwendoline. She was just twenty-one.

Towards two o'clock in the morning, when the musicians were nearly ready to pack up and go home, Sylvester's friend Philip McKenzie led his host aside. 'A terrible thing's happened, Michael. Mary's been robbed. Someone's rifled her handbag.' Mary was Philip's wife.

Michael was appalled. And his horror only grew when during the next half-hour it came to light that others too had had money stolen.

Mr Sylvester quickly telephoned Detective Inspector Boult. His hoarse voice was so insistent that it took Boult less than fifteen minutes to arrive. He had three men with him.

'But I can't understand it,' said Michael Sylvester. 'I've known every single one of the people here for years.'

'What about the waiters?' enquired Boult. 'How many were there?'

'I had five waiters,' answered Michael. 'And I also engaged the string quartet to play for us. All the same, the musicians can be eliminated. They played all evening without a break, and they didn't leave the veranda once. . . . Oh, there was one other person hired. A maid to be in attendance in the ladies' cloakroom.'

The police officer thought things over before making up his mind. 'You can tell the musicians they may go home, but I'd like everyone else to go into the house so that we can question them. Tell them that we're relying on their cooperation, and it's important for us to conduct a thorough investigation. I'm sure they'll understand. However, if a few of them are genuinely in a hurry to get away, my men will take their names and addresses and allow them to go. Of course, we may want to question them later if that proves to be necessary.'

Sylvester fluttered his hands in despair. 'Do you think you'll catch the thief?' he asked.

'We can only try,' answered Boult. 'The culprit or culprits may have had an accomplice who cleared off hours ago. But we must make a start somewhere.'

By this time there was widespread alarm and everyone started turning out pockets and handbags to discover exactly what was missing.

The interrogations began, conducted by Boult and one of his men. The other two policemen stood

by the front door to check those who declared they couldn't stay any longer.

Half an hour later, the list of those who had good reason to leave the house was presented to Detective Inspector Boult. Here it is:

Mr Christopher Lee, jeweller, and his wife: their children were alone at home and they didn't want to be absent too long.

Jack Bateman, antique dealer: he had to catch a plane to New York at six o'clock that morning.

Mr Michael Brown, banker, and his wife: the dog had been left in and they simply had to take it for a walk before they went to bed.

Ben Sole, trumpet player: it was all right for him to go. The inspector had already said that all the musicians could go home.

June Chester, no occupation: she was so upset that she simply had to go home and lie down.

Andrew Pickles, painter: he couldn't think of a good reason after all, so he changed his mind and stayed. (Boult crossed his name out immediately.)

Mel Santantonio, sales representative: his wife, who hadn't been able to come with him, expected him home by 3.30 at the latest.

Detective Inspector Boult read the list through twice before he looked up. The two constables were alarmed to see that he was scowling. He immediately went in search of Michael Sylvester, and his face showed clearly how annoyed he was. 'I'm sorry I haven't better news for you, sir, but my men have stupidly allowed the thief to leave the house. Don't worry, though. I promise you we'll catch him all right. Now that we know who he is, it's only a question of time. Good morning, sir.'

Who is the villain, according to Detective Inspector Boult?

17 · The road through Rushton Forest

The shortest way from Dillon to Earlbrook was through Rushton Forest. You could save at least fifteen minutes if you took that road, but there was one disadvantage: it was in a very bad state and was full of potholes. It was almost deserted during the week, but it was different on Saturdays and Sundays. Then it was very busy with people out for the day, especially cyclists and hikers. Late one Friday morning, Tony Masters, assistant to the head ranger, came out of a side path to cross the forest road. But the moment he reached it he braked hard and his moped came to an abrupt halt. Barely fifty metres away he saw a light grey car. And four paces from it lay a bicycle. Between the car and the bike was a man.

Masters knew who the man was, even though he was lying face down with his head turned away. He was Joe Walters, single, thirty-nine years old, and the accountant and chief cashier at the Earlbrook brickworks.

Masters guessed immediately what must have happened. Walters had clearly been mugged. The bloodstain on the back of his head left no room for

doubt on that score. Besides, there was an empty money bag by his side, and on it was the name of the nearest bank.

The young forester called Walters' name twice. There was no reaction. So Masters jumped on his moped and rode as fast as the machine would carry him to the nearest forestry hut where he would find a telephone.

It was about 11 am when Sergeant Collins and his experts arrived on the scene together with an ambulance. Meanwhile, Walters had recovered consciousness. His face was twisted with pain as he told his story. He had drawn the weekly wages for the Earlbrook brickworks from the bank in Dillon, as he did every Friday. As he left the bank he saw that someone had double parked, so that his own car was hemmed in. As a result, he had had to wait a good half an hour until the other driver returned. It was to make up at least in part for this lost time that he had taken the short cut through Rushton Forest. The workers at the brickyard expected to be paid by eleven o'clock every week. As for the attack itself, he made the following statement:

As I came round the bend I saw that the forest road was blocked by a cycle lying across it. I slowed down, stopped, and jumped out of the car to pull the bike out of the way. As I did so, I suddenly heard a noise behind me, but before I could so much as turn to discover what it was, I felt a tremendous blow on my head and I suppose it knocked me out completely.'

Sergeant Collins stroked his chin. 'Where exactly was the cash and how much was there?' he asked thoughtfully.

'I had £15,000 with me, and it was in a bank money bag, which I had put inside my briefcase.'

'And where was the briefcase?'

'On the front passenger seat.'

Collins made some notes while Walters fingered the plaster on the back of his head.

'And you can't give us any description of the attacker or attackers?'

Walters shook his head. 'All I saw was that the man wore a stocking mask and a pair of fawn gloves, leather ones.'

The sergeant nodded. The experts measuring the various tracks had finished by this time and Collins told Walters: 'You'd better come with me to headquarters and we'll get you to sign a formal statement.'

Two hours later, as Joe Walters signed the document containing his account of the mugging, Collins eyed him with a wry smile. And when he spoke, his words were bleak. 'We're keeping you in detention, Walters, at least for the present. Once you confess where the money is now and who your accomplice was, we can take it from there. In the meantime, the best thing you can do is to think over the ridiculous pack of lies you've been telling us.'

What was the tell-tale flaw in Walters' story that showed Sergeant Collins the mugging was a put-up job?

18 · The door-to-door salesman

The twenty-second of May was a date that Mrs Lynch was likely to remember for a long time. The day began well enough. The twins, Simon and Caroline, were going on a school outing, which meant that they wouldn't be home for lunch. It was a good opportunity for Mrs Lynch to have her hair permed, so she made an appointment at the hairdresser's for 11.30 am.

Mrs Lynch knew she would have to hurry if she was to get all the housework done in time. But before long, everything seemed to go wrong. She simply couldn't get on with all she had to do.

The first caller was Mrs Allen, her next-door neighbour. Mrs Allen was very upset as she explained that her married daughter, who lived fifty kilometres away, had been taken ill suddenly, and Mrs Allen simply had to go and see her. She'd be away for several days. If Mrs Lynch would kindly look after Hoppy, the canary, and water the house-plants, she'd be very grateful. As she left, she pressed her front door key into Mrs Lynch's hand.

Next, the phone rang. It was Caroline. No, there was nothing wrong, but Caroline wanted to tell her mother how the school outing was going, and everything they had done so far in the country.

At ten past ten the doorbell rang for the second time. A door-to-door salesman wanted to demonstrate the latest kitchen food processor.

At eleven o'clock another salesman stood on the doorstep. He tried to get her to buy one of his rugs.

And at twenty past eleven when she already had her coat on, yet a third young man appeared, who wanted her to place a regular order for some magazine or other, for which he would be paid a commission.

Towards three o'clock in the afternoon Mrs Lynch returned home from the hairdresser's only to find that the house had been broken into. The burglars had taken all her jewellery, some cash, an

expensive camera, as well as a valuable pair of binoculars.

Her neighbour's front door key had also disappeared. It turned out later that the thief must have known that Mrs Allen too was absent, for he took the opportunity to go through all the drawers and cupboards next door as well. The only thing that had been overlooked was a Post Office Savings Book, but that must have been pure chance.

When Sergeant Simpson was called to the house, he asked Mrs Lynch to tell him in great detail what had happened that morning, and particularly to try and recall her conversations with the three door-to-door salesmen.

It came as a surprise to Mrs Lynch to hear the officer's explanation. 'I'm sure that one of the three was the intruder, and that he belongs to a gang. It seems likely that you yourself as good as let him in. ... All the same, if you can give us a helpful description, I hope we'll soon catch him.'

Here are extracts from the three conversations that took place that morning. The culprit is revealed quite clearly:

The food processor salesman: 'Good morning, madam, I'd like to demonstrate our brand new multi-purpose food processor. No, no, it won't take a minute. ... But madam, there's plenty of time before eleven thirty. It's not nearly that ... I'm sure you'll never regret buying one. ... You can show it to your husband later even if he isn't in now. By that time you'll have discovered how useful it is. ... I'd be delighted to come back this evening, then. ... Oh well, if you're really not interested. Pity, I must say. . . . In that case I'll call on your neighbour. . . . She's not at home you say? . . . I see . . . for a few days. . . . Dear, dear, it isn't my lucky day, it seems!'

The carpet salesman: 'Look at the quality, madam, you won't get a rug like this at such a bargain price anywhere in town. . . . It's a once in a lifetime opportunity. . . . It's dirt cheap, and such a beautiful design. . . . You can't turn it down . . . let me make a suggestion. Allow me to put it down in your lounge, madam, and if you don't care for it in position, I'll roll it up and go. . . . Really, madam, your hairdresser won't run away, but if I go elsewhere and you hear that someone else has snapped it up, you'll regret it for years to come. . . . Oh well, all I can say is that you're the loser madam, I do assure you.'

The magazine salesman: 'May I ask you which magazines you take, madam . . . ? No, I'm not being inquisitive, but there's no point in offering you those you read already. . . . It won't take you a moment to see our range; fashion weeklies, illustrated monthlies. . . . Would your husband be interested in our sports or motoring magazines . . . ? I could easily come back this evening if you prefer. . . . In that case I can only apologise for disturbing you. Good morning!'

Which of these three conversations suggest that the man might come back and burgle the two houses?

19 · Looking for a scapegoat

For days now, John Lowe had felt exasperated whenever he caught sight of the deep scratch running from front to rear along the right-hand side of his brand new car.

He knew exactly how it had happened. He had parked in the big basement car-park at the cinema, and the fact that the damage was entirely his own fault galled him day after day. For John Lowe was the kind of person who always tried to put the blame on someone else.

That evening, though, there had been no one else about when he'd grazed the side of the car against a steel barrier. And since it was all his own fault he would have to foot the bill for the repair. And that went against the grain with mean Mr Lowe.

Having thought about it for three days, he came to a particularly unkind decision. He would find a scapegoat, some totally innocent person whom he could accuse of having scratched his car.

John Lowe's first step was to look for a street which would serve his purpose. He found a one-way street named Vernon Terrace, a narrow thoroughfare where parking was allowed.

Next morning, a Thursday, he set out early to carry out his plan. He parked his car, then parked himself! That's to say, he hid behind an advertisement hoarding and lay in wait for a suitable victim.

At 11.05, the moment arrived. A medium-sized delivery van turned into Vernon Terrace and Mr Lowe wrote down its registration number. Half an hour later, he entered the local police station, where an elderly sergeant asked him what he wanted. And John Lowe began his tale of woe.

'It was like this, officer. About nine o'clock this morning, I parked my car in Vernon Terrace. Then I did some shopping and I had to call at the bank. When I returned to get my car at 11.20, I found that a delivery van had scraped against it and made a deep scratch all along the right-hand side. It's a brand new Granada. I've only had it a fortnight.'

The sergeant was most sympathetic. 'Bad driving manners!' he nodded, and he sounded really angry. 'People dash off without a word for fear of losing their no claims bonus on the insurance policy. Were there any witnesses?'

Lowe shook his head. 'No, unfortunately.'

'I'm afraid it will be almost impossible to trace a van like that. You've no idea how many there are in a town like this.'

John Lowe now played his trump card. He sprang to his feet, pulled a slip of paper out of his pocket and flourished it in the sergeant's face. 'I was able to get his number, though. Here it is!'

The police officer beamed. 'Good. I'll get someone to check it on the computer and in a few minutes we'll know who owns the van.'

He took the receiver off the hook then suddenly replaced it. The friendly smile had gone and his eyes glared. 'I see! You're lying! You're looking for a scapegoat, someone you can blame for the damage to your car which was probably caused by your own carelessness.' With a menacing frown he eyed Mr Lowe and paused a moment. Then he went on: 'And trying to make a false claim to a police officer is an offence.' John Lowe, as white as a sheet and weak at the knees, sat down heavily. . . .

By and large, this case is a clear one. All the same, what made the sergeant change his mind? How did he know that John Lowe's case wasn't genuine?

20 · The last customer

The clock over the bar counter at The Green Cockatoo stood at 3 a.m. Apart from the owner, George Brell, who was acting as barman, and a handful of regulars, the only customer present was a man who sat alone at a table. He held an empty brandy glass in one hand, and he stared into it with a sad expression on his face. He was very drunk. He was about forty, and the clothes he wore were both expensive and fashionable.

'A ... a ... nother one!' he called, slurring his words.

Brell walked over from the bar to refill the glass.

'That's the last one, monsieur,' he said as he poured, but the man seemed to think the remark was meant for someone else. As he had done throughout the evening, he paid for the drink from a wad of notes in his trouser pocket. 'Okay ... keep the change.'

It was a fifty-franc note, as Brell saw, but he pocketed it without a word. His motto was that the customer is always right.

By 3.15 the only customer left was the lonely figure at the table. 'Just one more!' he insisted with the typical obstinacy of a man who is drunk. Reluctantly, Brell crossed the room. 'This really *is* the last one. I mean it,' he said firmly. With a curt 'Thanks!' he pocketed the note he was offered, a twenty-franc one this time. The last customer downed the glass of brandy at a gulp and, without any warning, collapsed across the table. A moment later he started snoring.

Brell swore under his breath. 'That's the last straw!' he fumed. He thought hard before returning to the man and shaking him roughly several times.

There was no response.

Brell took hold of the man under the arms and, taking all his weight, dragged him towards the door, walking backwards. Without turning, he pushed open the door with one foot.

Outside in the street he carefully propped his ex-customer, who had now sunk into a kind of stupor, against the wall of the building.

Seven hours later.

In the flat above the Green Cockatoo, George Brell sat facing Inspector Malle. 'You say you've come to see me about one of my customers, Inspector?'

Malle had no time to waste. 'Monsieur Jules Arcide has been to the police station. He accuses you of theft.'

Brell's face was a blank. He had no idea what the inspector was talking about. 'I don't know anyone by the name of Arcide,' he said with a shrug. 'It's the first time I've ever heard it.'

'He was one of your customers yesterday.'

Brell gave a laugh. 'At a rough guess, I'd say I know at most ten per cent of my customers by name. And that ten per cent doesn't include anyone called Arcide, on my word of honour.'

'It's possible that the gentleman in question had had a little too much to drink. Be that as it may, he found himself at about five o'clock this morning leaning against the wall outside your bar. He says you stole all the money he had in his wallet. More than twelve thousand francs.'

George Brell stared at the inspector. After a long silence he jumped to his feet. 'Now I know who you mean,' he exclaimed angrily. 'He was my last customer. I couldn't get rid of him! He paid for all his drinks from notes in his trouser pocket. ... Let me tell you, Inspector, this is a bar I keep here in Nice, not a nursing-home for people who don't even know when they've had too much to drink!'

The inspector raised his hand. 'There's no need to get excited, monsieur. I suppose any passer-by might have helped himself to the missing wallet. But Monsieur Arcide has named you personally, so we have no choice but to follow up his complaint. Naturally you could sue him later if you think fit. But your best line would be to tell me exactly what happened.'

'As you please,' nodded George Brell, 'but there isn't much to tell. I can't say precisely what time the fellow wandered in. At a rough guess I'd say it was between ten o'clock and midnight. All I know is that he drank one brandy after another. I usually close the bar at about 3 am, and I'd intended to do just that this morning, but there were a few regulars who weren't in a hurry to go home, so I waited.... Once they'd gone, only this Monsieur Marcide....'

'Arcide,' corrected the police officer.

'Okay, Arcide. He was the only person left. I'd already sent Pierre, my waiter, home, and I was serving myself. I locked the outer door as soon as Pierre and the others had gone.... You never know, do you? This fellow asked me for just one more. You know how it is, the way they always beg for another drink when they've had too much already. But I gave in and poured him a small brandy, which he drank. Then without any warning he collapsed across the table and started snoring. I was fed up, believe me. All I wanted was to get to bed. So I dragged him outside as carefully as I could and propped him up against the wall. And that's the truth!'

'Very good,' said Inspector Malle. 'At present I can't prove anything one way or the other. All the same, I'd be glad if you'd come with me to the police station so that I can take a statement from you.'

'As you please,' agreed Brell, with a marked lack of enthusiasm. As he put on his jacket he asked sourly: 'If anyone can tell me how to earn an honest living without being wrongly accused of theft and other crimes, I'll change my job tomorrow!'

'I'll think about it,' promised the inspector with the ghost of a smile on his face.

We can't prove whether or not George Brell had robbed his customer any more than Inspector Malle can. But we know for certain that he told the inspector an untruth in one particular. And this in turn makes us wonder if he didn't rob his customer after all. What was the lie Brell told the inspector?

21 · A case for Perry Clifton

It was Sunday.

Perry Clifton, the London store detective, sat in his Norwood flat. One of his hobbies was mending watches and clocks, and he was busy tinkering with an old alarm clock when the doorbell rang.

Perry opened the door.

'My name is Mrs Dawson,' the caller said. 'You *are* Mr Clifton, aren't you?'

Clifton nodded. The short, plump lady before him with her jolly but shrewd face struck him as a familiar figure.

'I live across the road.'

'Of course!' Perry slapped his forehead. 'I know you now. You're the lady from the launderette! What can I do for you, Mrs Dawson?'

The lady leaned forward and lowered her voice. 'People say you're a detective. If it's true, there's something I'd like to discuss with you,' she whispered in her softest voice.

'Please come in then,' said Clifton, motioning her indoors.

'Well,' she began after a moment's hesitation, 'At first I was going to go to the police, but my John –

he's my husband – said they'd laugh at me. It was his idea to come to you instead. So here I am!' She underlined her last remark with a firm nod of her head.

Perry smiled gravely, trying to look as serious as his caller seemed to be. 'As you say, here you are. Won't you tell me what it is that alarmed you and Mr Dawson so much?'

'Of course, but I don't want you to think that my John's alarmed. Nothing rattles him,' she insisted, determined to remove any misunderstanding. 'He never gets excited! The other day when we were shopping, I missed my footing and fell full length in the street.' Her eyes flashed and her voice grew louder. 'And do you know what my John said?'

Perry shook his head politely.

'He said: "That's all right, Mary, if you feel like lying down don't let me stop you! Stay where you are. I'll be back soon!" That's what he said, did John. And off he went to The Black Lion for a pint, leaving me to pick myself up as best I could. That's my John for you. He works on the railway, an engine driver.'

'Why didn't your John come with you now?' interrupted Perry Clifton in an attempt to stem the woman's flow of words.

'Oh, he couldn't do that. He's on the late shift today. On the line to Exeter, you know.... Now, what was I saying?' Mrs Dawson tried hard to think, propping her head on her hand and frowning for all she was worth.

'You wanted my advice, Mrs Dawson,' said Perry patiently.

His visitor laughed, stretched out one hand and cried: 'That's right!' Then moving her head closer to Perry's she again lowered her voice.

'Just imagine,' she began. 'I was in the kitchen cooking the dinner when there was a sudden bang. Did you hear it?'

'When?'

'Earlier on, about twelve.'

'Yes, I did. It was an RAF supersonic fighter.'

Again Mrs Dawson's eyes flashed, this time with

indignation. 'There ought to be a law against it! The thoughtless lads, they should punish them severely. I got such a fright that I dropped the gas-lighter in the pan of soup simmering on the cooker. And when I finally managed to fish it out, there was a pigeon sitting on my kitchen table.'

'Really? A pigeon?'

'Yes, Mr Clifton, a carrier pigeon. My John noticed right away that there was a tiny capsule tied to its leg.'

'It sounds as if the supersonic bang frightened it too, so that it took refuge through the nearest open window. Did you let it go again?'

'Yes, I did. But not before my John had had a look at the message it was carrying.'

Mrs Dawson's hand slipped into her handbag and, with the expression of an actress making a grand entrance, she held out a piece of paper to Perry Clifton. 'My John copied it down, word for word.'

Clifton felt an odd tingle down his spine as he took the scrap of paper from the woman. Then he read it aloud softly:

'Copenhagen, 12 September.

Dear Jan,

Arrived safely and got in touch with B. immediately. He thinks the Guilder notes have come out very well and will buy them from us for £10,000. I'm just off to Stockholm. All the best. Piet.'

Mrs Dawson stood up, eyeing the detective expectantly. 'Well? What do you say to that?'

Clifton's face looked serious. 'You certainly had

the right idea, Mrs Dawson. It clearly refers to forged banknotes, Dutch ones.'

'And what happens now?' she asked, her eyes gleaming with excitement.

'You'd better go home, and don't breathe a word about it to a soul. I'll go and see if I can sniff out this mysterious Jan.'

'But I thought . . .' objected Mrs Dawson.

Perry Clifton laid a gentle hand on the woman's shoulder and his voice conveyed clearly that John's wife was now in some danger. 'Do you want to risk your life, Mrs Dawson? These people will be ruthless if they're cornered. They're a law unto themselves. How would you like to find yourself kidnapped and locked in a cellar . . . ? You don't want your John to spend months and months looking for you, now do you?'

All at once, Mrs Dawson was in a great hurry. And from his window Perry Clifton could see her glancing back anxiously over her shoulder as she made tracks for her safe little flat above the launderette.

Thirty-six hours later, Perry Clifton had solved the case. The man named Jan lived in an old house at the end of Bolton Street. From the pavement, Perry could see clearly the double entrance to the pigeon loft tucked away under the gable of the dingy grey house.

Shortly after six that evening, Detective Inspector Scott and two of his men arrived from Scotland Yard and stood in front of the house.

By twenty to seven, it was all over.

The Special Branch officers found printing-presses and forged notes in the cellar. All in all, they would have amounted to £50,000 worth of currency if they had been genuine.

When the trial took place a few months later, Jan van Kampen, born in Amsterdam, could hardly believe that it was a pigeon that had cooked his goose!

The difficult problem for you to solve is this: What was the country of origin of the pigeon in the case?

22 · The Queen of Pickpockets

Her name was Lena, Lena Lang, and she was considered the Queen of Pickpockets. Only once had she been caught, and that was when the victim whose wallet she had deftly extracted from an inner pocket turned out to be a member of the Crime Squad.

Lena's success was due to one particular skill: she was a master – or rather a mistress – in the art of disguise. Whether she dressed up as a beggar, as a smartly dressed woman, as a priest or as a postman, her disguise was always foolproof. No one ever suspected that behind the costume lurked Lena, Queen of Pickpockets.

It was 27 September, a memorable day, as Lena Lang discovered to her cost. During the past week she'd fixed her attention on the main railway station of a large town. For four days running she had been so successful that she decided to continue there for a fifth day, this same 27 September.

What she did not know was that many of her thefts had been reported. As a result, a massive police presence had been arranged for that very

BANK
GENTS
LADIES

day. No fewer than ten railway policemen, as well as fourteen regular officers in plain clothes, were dotted around the station ready to pounce.

This September morning, Lena Lang had chosen to dress up as a man in Bavarian national costume – leather shorts, a deerstalker hat with a jaunty tuft from a goat's beard, and a knobbly walking-stick. She stuck a bushy beard on her chin and she held a pipe in her mouth. The disguise was complete. And then things happened.

She had 'accidentally' bumped into a well-dressed gentleman, with the result that his bulging wallet was now in her possession. Suddenly Lena became aware of a pair of eyes boring into her back. She turned slightly and from the corner of her eye she picked out a harmless-looking man behind her, a quiet type of person in an ordinary grey suit. She strolled past him as if nothing were amiss. But she knew that he was following her.

It was then that Lena Lang made the mistake of her life.

To shake off her pursuer who, she suspected, had seen her stealing the money, she decided she would have to slip away somewhere safe. And where safer than the lavatory? Unfortunately for her, this only confirmed the suspicions of the plain clothes man in grey.

When she appeared at the lavatory exit about six minutes later, a pair of handcuffs was smartly clapped on her wrists.

Why was it a mistake for Lena Lang to try to hide where she did?

Solutions

The high-rise robbery, page 7.

It can safely be assumed that the pipe on the table was not one of the art treasures on sale at the Gallery Lacoste! So having found it, the police knew at once that Smoky Sam was likely to be one of the culprits.

The castle of the red gorillas, page 13.

1 According to the story, the room in which the meal was served had hundreds of tallow candles burning. Yet when the old gentleman switched off the light, everything was said to be in total darkness.
2 When it grew light next day, André Passou worked out that the room where he had spent the night was on the ground floor. Yet as he was driving away he is said to have looked up to the room on the second floor where he had been left alone with the seven scarlet gorillas.

Happy Easter! page 27.

It was Knut Bjorn who hadn't told the truth. His story was that he hadn't left his house since Saturday evening. But if that were true, how could he have lost his car keys in the snow? It didn't start snowing until Easter Sunday!

Dinner at the Zanzibar, page 32.

According to Oxter, he left his flat for the Hotel Zanzibar at 8 pm and he found that the safe in his office had been robbed at 9.15. He also said that it took him half an hour to drive to the restaurant and, it's safe to assume, the same time to return. Or one hour's travelling time all told.

In that case he had no more than a quarter of an hour to spare. Now Olaf Kellborn knew for a fact that dining at an expensive place like the Zanzibar would have taken longer than that. Paul's claim that he had ordered a meal, eaten it and discovered the burglary within a mere fifteen minutes couldn't have been true.

A red-hot tip, page 37.

Our friend Sandy had had too much to drink. Instead of breaking into number twenty-four King Henry Avenue, where the owner was away, he had cut the kitchen window of number twenty-six, where the owner was very much at home!

A road accident, page 42.

The accident occurred in April 1978. The date of birth shown in the driving licence was 19 March 1950, and Mr Shotter of Greene Brothers confirmed that Mr Hulbert had been on their staff for seventeen years.

From 1950 to 1978 is twenty-eight years. If you take seventeen years from 1978, the result would be that Mr Hulbert started work – and work that involved driving a car, what's more – in 1961, or in other words when he was only eleven years of age!

Chicken and mushroom pie, page 47.

It must have been Benson, the only one of the three who had his own telephone. You couldn't have devised a hoax that involved 'fixing' a tape-recording from a public call-box. Furthermore, he boasted that he used to enjoy playing about with tapes.

Dirty work at the car-park, page 51.

The driver of the Metro claimed that he had been away from the car-park for three hours or thereabouts. How then could he have known that a red Mercedes and a white Escort had been parked on either side of his car, since both had long since left, and had not arrived before he locked up the Metro at 7.45?

Frontier incident, page 56.

The drugs smugglers were in the dark green Opel with the German (Munich) number-plates. Only they could have known that there was a French-registered Fiat immediately ahead of them. And they were the only ones in a position to take advantage of the fact that the customs officers were concentrating all their attention on the suspect Fiat.

A dangerous game, page 60.

The battered light blue Mini was the lady's downfall. How could she have known how the burglars made their getaway, or what their car looked like, if she were tied to a chair, which in turn was tied to a kitchen pipe, and it took her two hours to free herself?

Chocolate Charlie, page 65.

Charlie Chuckles' big mistake was to forget his hat. He left it lying on a statuette at Chocorama. Tucked into the inside band, together with other important slips of paper, was his speeding ticket. So it was child's play for the police to trace him.

The stolen tune, page 70.

It was Frank Hilton, not Bobby Berg. James Gilbert's business trip had taken him to Detroit and Boston as well as Chicago. Only someone who had been in touch with the music publishers would have known for certain that their headquarters were in Chicago, and that that was where Gilbert would have gone to see them.

A message in code, page 75.

If you want to know what Hugh Wimpey was trying to tell his brother about his planned escape, you have only to read alternately one word from the start of the text and one word from the end. It reads as follows:

DAY	FOUR	NEXT	WEEK
FREEDOM	BID	HAVE	CAR
READY	TWO	BEFORE	TWELVE

Or, in plain language, he intended to escape the following Wednesday at 10 am.

Supersleuth, Swedish style, page 78.

There were four mistakes all told:

1 Gunnar walked sixty kilometres a week, not seventy. He didn't go into the village on Sundays.
2 A silent film couldn't have had the title *Murder on the Jumbo Jet*. There were no jumbo jets in those days.
3 Being a silent film, there couldn't have been a lisping voice nor could the intruder have listened spell-bound to the film.
4 Gunnar had had to leave his hearing-aid in town for repair. Without it, according to the text, he was completely deaf. So he couldn't have heard the noise of someone trying to open the front door with a key.

The widow from Australia, page 82.

During the conversation between Arthur Robbins and the woman who called herself Pamela Ferguson, the detective did not mention Oxford, the place where Jefferson Kirby committed the bank fraud. But when she was accused of being Diana Kirby and not an Australian widow, she protested that she had never been in Oxford in her life. She couldn't have admitted her guilt more plainly.

The birthday party, page 88.

The most suspicious name on the list, according to Detective Inspector Boult, was that of Ben Sole, the trumpet player. Although he was a musician, he couldn't have been playing on the veranda all evening, as the music was provided by four string players and the trumpet is a wind instrument.

The road through Rushton Forest, page 93.

Walters stated that he heard a noise when he got out of the car to clear the bicycle from the path, and that before he could even turn around he received a blow on the head which knocked him out. In that case, how could he declare that his attacker wore a stocking mask and fawn leather gloves, if he hadn't had time to see who it was before he passed out?

The door-to-door salesman, page 97.

The first one, the food processor salesman, arouses most suspicion. He was the only one who knew not just that Mrs Lynch was going to have her hair done, but also that her neighbour's house was empty as well. She didn't mention this to either of the other two callers.

Looking for a scapegoat, page 102.

John Lowe had said that he found his car was damaged when he returned to Vernon Terrace at 11.20. The sergeant became suspicious when the man presented him with the registration number of the van. If the damage had really been done in his absence, and there were no witnesses, how could he possibly have known the registration number of the van?

The last customer, page 106.

As Brell dragged the customer from the table, he didn't turn around when he reached the door but pushed it open with his foot. If he had locked the door after Pierre had gone, as he told the inspector, that would have been impossible.

A Case for Perry Clifton, page 112.

A carrier pigeon invariably returns to its own loft, so the answer must be England. Piet had sent the message by pigeon post, believing that this was the safest way of letting Jan know what had happened. But thanks to the Dawsons - and to Perry Clifton - he was very much mistaken.

The Queen of Pickpockets, page 118.

In the ordinary way it wouldn't have been at all suspicious if a woman went into a ladies' lavatory at a railway station. However, in the heat of the moment Lena Lang forgot that she was convincingly dressed as a man. How could it fail to arouse suspicion?